Look Good,
Feel Great
COOKBOOK

Look Good, Feel Great

COOKBOOK

Jenny Jones

Photography by Jenny Jones

Foreword by Donald Redhun, M.S.P.H., M.D.

WILEY

WILEY PUBLISHING, INC.

For general information about our other products and services, please contact our Customer Care Department within the United States at (800) 762-2974, outside the United States at (317) 572-3993 or fax (317) 572-4002.

Wiley also publishes its books in a variety of electronic formats. Some content that appears in print may not be available in electronic books. For more information about Wiley products, visit our web site at www.wiley.com.

LIBRARY OF CONGRESS CATALOGING-IN-PUBLICATION DATA

Jones, Jenny.
  Look good, feel great cookbook / Jenny Jones ; photography by Jenny Jones.
        p. cm.
  Includes index.
  ISBN-13: 978-0-7645-9958-3 (cloth)
  ISBN-10: 0-7645-9958-5 (cloth)
  1. Cookery. 2. Nutrition. I. Title.
  TX714.J65242 2006
  641.5'63—dc22
                                                              2005009404

Book design by Richard Oriolo

Printed in the United States of America
10 9 8 7 6 5 4 3 2 1

I dedicate this book

to the first and

best cook I ever knew,

my father, John.

Contents

Acknowledgments

I want to thank the love of my life, Denis, for his unconditional support as I baked, sautéed, and roasted my way through this book. As much as I love to cook there were days when I didn't love it quite as much and Denis was always there to help me laugh about it. Like the time I overbaked some muffins and he offered to call the NHL to see if they could use twelve extra hockey pucks. Denis was always there with a supportive word and he was fearless in eating whatever I put on his plate, even if it resembled sporting equipment. He also helped me pick my best photos when I couldn't decide.

Luckily for me, I have a housekeeper who loves to cook as much as I do. Antonia was a big help to me with her suggestions and tasting comments and a special thanks to her for ironing all those fabrics for my pictures. She also conquered mountains of dishes on a daily basis, always with a smile.

This book would not exist if not for the steadfast support of Mel Berger, my longtime friend and publishing agent at William Morris. When I called Mel to see if he thought this was a good idea I was prepared to have to sell him on my doing this book, but I never got the chance. He immediately said yes. "Just let me know when you're ready," he said. I knew right then that I would have the book I wanted, thanks to Mel.

Justin Schwartz, my editor and bicoastal email buddy, not only guided and educated me through this new territory but more importantly, he completely understood my vision. This was not going to be a traditional cookbook and he really got that. Justin made sure I was able to write the book my way, in my own language, and I'm very grateful for that.

I knew how important the cover of this book would be and it turned out even better than I expected. Art director Jeff Faust did a fantastic job on the design, and that awesome photo of me was taken by Los Angeles photographer Charles Bush. Charles's easygoing style really makes taking pictures fun. I also want to thank the best make-up artist I know, Earl Nicholson, for his gifted makeup work and Ricardo Santiago for working his magic on my hair. Earl and Ricardo worked with me on "The Jenny Jones Show" and came in all the way from Chicago to Los Angeles just to make me look good. Besides being stars at what they do they are also my sweetest friends.

Thanks also to my publicist, Leslie Garson, who kept finding new ways to promote my cooking, and to Wiley's Associate Director of Publicity, Gypsy Lovett, for a superb job in promoting this book. I also want to thank all of the team members at Wiley, some of whom I have never even met, for all of their efforts on behalf of this book.

And every time a friend or coworker raved about something I cooked it boosted my confidence and they unknowingly contributed to this book. Thanks to Dana, who loves my Beet-Cabbage Borscht; Matthew, who raves about my lemon squares; Tracey, who's still talking about my sweet potato chocolate cake; Rick and Cheryl, who refused to go home without my Roasted Tomato Soup recipe; Barbara, who refuses to share my peanut butter cookies; Yelena, who can't get enough of my pumpkin chocolate chip muffins; Kerrie, who lives for my meringues; and Zazi, who says my brownies are the best she's ever had. Thank you all for contributing, although indirectly, to this book.

And finally, I'd like to thank the first cook I ever knew, my dad, John, for encouraging me to help out in the kitchen, and for a lifetime of inspired home cooking. I share his passion for food and know that had he lived to see this book he would have been very proud.

Foreword

These days, many Americans are making poor dietary choices, eating excessive portions, and not getting enough exercise. Because of the fast-paced lives we lead, or just the lack of desire to prepare our own food, we have seen an explosion in the popularity of fast food restaurants over the last few decades. The menu choices are inexpensive, and there is always a restaurant conveniently located nearby your home. Many of these companies spend a fortune on advertising to lure adults and their children. Unfortunately, this has resulted in the consumption of a diet high in saturated fats, added sugars, refined grains, and worthless calories. We now face an obesity epidemic throughout America. Saturated fats, sweets, and alcohol are foods we should limit or avoid. Everyone should eat a "balanced" diet, incorporating a certain number of foods from the five basic food groups every day.

Beyond a balanced diet, making specific choices about what we eat can have an even greater impact on health and disease prevention. Most of us are aware of the many health benefits associated with eating fruits and vegetables. Scientists have discovered that in addition to their vitamin, mineral, and fiber content, fresh produce contains naturally occurring substances called phytochemicals. These compounds act to protect the plants and also give them their specific color, scent, and flavor. Increasing evidence suggests that these phytochemicals, also referred to as phytonutrients, may have multiple benefits to humans. By eating fruits and vegetables from each color group, you can get a full range of phytonutrients, some of which are believed to reduce the risk of cancer (antioxidant phytochemicals)

and heart disease, while others may boost our immunity. Some phyto-chemicals help our vision (improve night vision and reduce the risk of developing cataracts and macular degeneration), can prevent prostate problems, help reduce the risk of osteoporosis, and may reduce or slow memory loss. Thus, the daily consumption of fruits and vegetables will help us achieve good health and provide energy today and additionally will provide many long-term health benefits.

Having practiced Internal Medicine for over twenty years and having had the privilege to care for thousands of individuals, I can honestly state that the connection between diet, exercise, and health cannot be underestimated. Just as people make conscious decisions to brush their teeth or wear seatbelts in a car, they should get in the habit of eating all types of vegetables and fruits on a daily basis. Incorporating specific ingredients in recipes and foods in our diet can help reduce our risk of developing health problems in the future. Making sensible and educated decisions about the ingredients and specific foods you eat can give you more energy, more vitality, and have a profound influence on the rest of your life.

—Donald Rebhun, M.S.P.H., M.D.

June 2005

Donald Rebhun, M.S.P.H., M.D., is a practicing Internal Medicine specialist in the San Fernando Valley in Southern California. In addition to his active clinical practice, he is a Regional Medical Director for HealthCare Partners Medical Group and sits on the Board of Directors for the California Association of Physician Groups (CAPG) and the Integrated HealthCare Association. While away from work, he loves playing tennis, music, and spending time with his wife and four children.

Introduction

Fruits and Vegetables Can Save Your Life

Everyone's talking about it. Even *Time* magazine wrote that fruits and vegetables "aren't just good for you, they are so good for you they can save your life." There's a new science emerging, and the latest research has shown that certain foods high in antioxidants can dramatically reduce your risk of getting ailments such as arthritis, type II diabetes, certain cancers, hypertension, stroke, osteoporosis, high cholesterol, high blood pressure, macular degeneration, cataracts, obesity, diverticular disease, Alzheimer's, circulatory problems, and heart disease. There are thousands of "micronutrients" in foods, many of which have yet to be identified, but we already know that they can do everything from improve your memory to strengthen your immune system, and actually slow the aging process. Who wouldn't want that?

Foods like blueberries, beans, oats, pumpkins, mangoes, walnuts, peppers, spinach, and tomatoes are just some of the antioxidant superstars. It seems that every week there is a new article, discovery, or research study about the health benefits of eating certain foods, and it just makes sense to find ways to incorporate as many of these superfoods into your everyday cooking as possible. That's exactly what I have done. My old Chicken and Rice became Chicken and Rice with Peppers, which now might help protect me from cataracts and heart disease. My old Chocolate Cake became Sweet Potato Chocolate Cake, which now might protect my eyes, lungs, heart, and immune system. And by simply adding oat bran to my meat loaf it can now help lower my cholesterol.

How do I know all this? I've been studying and reading about nutrition all my life. My office is full of books on health and nutrition, and I always seek out the latest information in magazines, newspapers, and on the Internet. In planning for this book, I began cataloging all the information I could find on which foods might actually prevent disease and improve our overall health. Then I set out to give all my personal recipes a makeover by making them even healthier than they already were. There must be something to eating healthy food because I have yet to take a sick day in over forty years.

The 4-1-1 on Antioxidants

Here it is in a nutshell: Antioxidants do exactly what the word says. They are the "anti" to oxidation. You know when you cut an apple and it turns brown? That's oxidation. The process of oxidation is essential to human life but too much of it creates "free radicals" in our bodies. These are the bad boys that cause degenerative disease and aging. So the good guys (antioxidants) beat up the bad guys (free radicals). The result is you can live a longer, healthier, disease-free life.

Antioxidants include vitamin C, vitamin E, beta-carotene (a form of vitamin A), and selenium, plus a bunch of hard-to-pronounce phytonutrients (meaning nutrients found in plants) like carotenoids and polyphenols. You don't need to know all the names, but just remember that they are mostly found in different colored fruits and vegetables and the deeper the color, the higher the antioxidant level. That's why they tell us to eat five servings a day of fruits and vegetables. And by choosing the ones highest in antioxidants your health is sure to benefit. Antioxidants also occur in tea, nuts, seeds, certain oils, whole grains, fish, legumes, beans, red wine, and even dark chocolate—Yippee!

Below I have listed some of the important foods we all need to eat along with some, but not all, of their health benefits:

AVOCADOS
- provide heart-healthy oil and potassium
- may protect the heart by keeping cholesterol in check

BANANAS
- provide fiber, potassium, and magnesium
- good for lowering blood pressure and cholesterol

BEANS
- provide iron, calcium, phosphorus, and soluble fiber
- lower cholesterol and suppress appetite to help control weight

BEETS
- provide vitamin C, beta-carotene, folic acid, polyphenols, potassium, lycopene, and fiber
- may protect against colon cancer, heart disease, diabetes, asthma, stroke, and birth defects, as well as help detoxify the liver

BLUEBERRIES
- provide fiber, vitamin A, vitamin C, vitamin E, folic acid, calcium, potassium, polyphenols, carotenoids, and indoles
- may help prevent cancer, heart disease, memory loss, birth defects, bone loss, diabetes, Alzheimer's, cataracts, and macular degeneration

BROCCOLI
- provides vitamin C, vitamin A, folic acid, calcium, and potassium
- may protect against cancer, heart disease, cataracts, macular degeneration, and osteoporosis, as well as strengthen the immune system

CANTALOUPE
- provides beta-carotene
- may protect the eyes, heart, and lungs and reduce the risk of cancer

CARROTS	■ provide beta-carotene
	■ (same as cantaloupe)
CITRUS FRUITS	■ provide vitamin C, pectin, and fiber
	■ may boost the immune system and reduce the risk of cancer
CRUCIFEROUS VEGETABLES	■ includes cabbage, broccoli, Brussels sprouts, kale, collards, mustard greens, bok choy, radish, turnip, and rutabaga
	■ contain indoles
	■ research strongly suggests protection from cancer
FISH	■ provides omega-3 fatty acids
	■ may reduce the risk of stroke, heart disease, and arthritis
GARLIC AND ONIONS	■ contain allicin
	■ may prevent cancer, blood clots, and heart disease
MANGOES	■ provide beta-carotene, vitamin C, vitamin E, fiber, and potassium
	■ may reduce blood pressure and protect your eyes, lungs, and heart, as well as reduce the risk of cancer
NUTS	■ contain omega-3 fatty acids
	■ known to lower cholesterol and the risk of heart disease
OATMEAL	■ provides selenium, potassium, B vitamins, iron, and soluble fiber
	■ known to lower cholesterol and reduce the risk of heart disease
PAPAYA	■ provides vitamin A, vitamin C, potassium, and pectin
	■ may lower cholesterol and blood pressure and aid digestion
PEPPERS	■ includes red, green, yellow, and orange bell peppers as well as chile peppers
	■ contain many antioxidants
	■ may reduce the risk of cancer, heart disease, and macular degeneration; peppers also help to burn fat
PUMPKIN	■ provides beta-carotene
	■ may protect the eyes, heart, and lungs, and reduce the risk of cancer

- provides beta-carotene, lutein, iron, vitamin C, vitamin E, and potassium
- may protect against macular degeneration, cataracts, osteoporosis, birth defects, heart disease, and cancer

- provide vitamin A, vitamin C, vitamin E, calcium, and fiber
- may strengthen the immune system and protect your heart, lungs, eyes, and bones
- may reduce blood pressure and the risk of cancer

- contains polyphenols
- may protect against heart disease and cancer as well as strengthen the capillaries, urinary tract, and immune system

- provide lycopene
- may protect against prostate cancer, heart disease, memory loss, macular degeneration, and even wrinkles

About My Cooking

I love to cook. It's something I've been doing all my life, and when you do something you truly enjoy, and you do it almost every day, you get pretty good at it. My dad was the cook in the family and I enjoyed helping out, but I didn't get serious about cooking until I left home at the age of seventeen. I think I missed my dad's home cooking.

I bought some cookbooks and learned to cook and bake. Before long I began instinctively adapting recipes to make them healthier. This was back in the '60s when people like me were called "Health Food Nuts." Back then health food stores were hard to find, and when you did find one it usually had that weird smell.

Nowadays health food stores are everywhere, and as people become more nutritionally aware many supermarkets are responding by adding health food sections. There's clearly more and more evidence that eating healthy, well-balanced meals is the best way to look great and feel great.

As a struggling comedian I supported myself by cooking for others out of my home. I got so busy I couldn't keep up and had to hire a friend to help. I shopped for groceries at night, cooked all day, and then delivered all the orders on my bike. When I landed my syndicated daytime talk show, the only perk I asked for was a full kitchen in my dressing room, where I cooked my own breakfast and lunch every day.

I prefer simple, home-style food that's not fancy or complicated, and I believe it's the way most people like to eat. I call it reality cooking because the reality is, I am not going to eat tofu. Ditto for rice cakes. When people are eating tofu or rice cakes they don't look happy. But pizza makes people smile. That's how I want to feel every time I eat. . . and I do.

Of course, brown rice is more nutritious than white rice, and whole-wheat pasta is better for you than the one that tastes good. . . but the truth is, if we don't enjoy it, we are probably not going to eat it. I like the same things everybody else does—mac 'n' cheese, spaghetti and meatballs, cookies and cakes—and since I refuse to give them up, I've dedicated myself to making all the things I love as healthy as possible. It's not perfect, but it is realistic. I just took my favorite foods and gave them a Jenny Jones Recipe Makeover.

Here is what you will find in this book:

- No fancy sauces
- No exotic ingredients
- Most ingredients are available at the supermarket
- Some ingredients are available at health food stores
- Recipes that don't taste like "health food"
- Easy to follow, step-by-step instructions
- Recipes that are low in saturated fat
- Desserts that are low in sugar and saturated fat
- Liberal use of healthy olive and canola oils
- Minimal use of butter
- Recipes that are high in antioxidants
- Shopping lists with every recipe
- Recipe photos all taken by me at my home

About My Photography

I can hardly believe that I did all the photography for this book, but it turned out to be so much fun. My love of taking pictures started when I received a 35mm camera for Christmas, though I hardly used it for two years. It had so many buttons and dials, and I was intimidated. Then came the big revelation: If I set it on "auto," all I had to do was press one button and I had my picture. Wow! Who knew? Then I went crazy. Anything that moved, I grabbed my camera. . . butterflies, ladybugs, spiders, mosquitoes, it didn't matter. With my macro lens it was my own personal close-up nature show.

When I decided to write this book, it was only natural that I take the pictures for it. This way I got to combine my two favorite things to do: cooking and photography. But nature photography and food

photography are not the same. I needed a studio, props, and, as I soon discovered, lights, which I found at the local camera store. My dining room has the best natural light (big windows), so I turned it into a photo studio, got my 35mm camera, and started practicing. After about twenty trips to the one-hour photo, I sprung for a digital camera. I found some props around the house and others at antique malls, second-hand shops, and thrift stores. Most of the "tablecloths" are pieces of material I bought at the fabric store.

Each picture took anywhere from twenty minutes to five or six hours, when I couldn't get it just right. Every session started the same way, with me wandering around the house looking for props. Every room, not just the kitchen, had something I could use. Candle holders, picture frames, clothing, tchotchkes—they're all here in the pictures. I estimate that I took about 25,000 pictures in preparing for this book.

My photos are all exactly as I took them, no retouching, no Photoshop, no alterations whatsoever. I've included a line or two with each photo in order to share the whole experience.

Time to Get Healthy

Diets are So Last Year

You've seen them come and go. Remember the grapefruit diet? How about the cabbage soup diet? Protein powder? Beverly Hills? Juicing? Fasting? Carbs-good. Carbs-bad. Enough, already! Diets are done; they're over. Most people who diet to lose weight and then stop "dieting" will gain back the weight, and often more, because their metabolism has slowed down. Every time another trendy diet bites the dust it always comes back to balanced meals. Eating healthy balanced meals including lean protein, fiber, the right carbohydrates, and well-chosen fats will keep your blood sugar and metabolism regulated to help burn stored fat for long-term weight loss. And if you include

high antioxidant fruits and vegetables, you could also be saving your life.

*P*eople often ask me how it is that I never get sick. No colds. No flu. Nothing. It could be because I do my best to follow these rules:

1. **Read food labels.** Never buy a grocery item without reading the ingredient list. If you can't pronounce it, don't eat it.

2. **Avoid "partially hydrogenated" anything.** That means it contains trans fats, which are worse for you than butter. Trans fats can raise your cholesterol and contribute to heart disease.

3. **Keep snacking.** Eat smaller meals and snacks throughout the day and avoid big meals with huge portions. You'll stay thinner and live longer.

4. **Are those nuts in your pocket?** I never leave the house without a "snack-pack," a little antioxidant-filled baggie of walnuts, almonds, raisins, and other dried fruit.

5. **Think five-a-day.** You really should try to eat five servings of fruits and vegetables every day, but hey, even one is better than none. Good news: Even jams and fruit spreads count.

6. **Avoid soft drinks.** Read the labels. A typical cola has around forty milligrams of sugar—that's almost $1/4$ cup!

7. **Fast food? Keep driving.** I haven't been to a fast food restaurant in years. This will make the biggest difference in your health.

8. **Drink green tea.** This may be the ultimate health-promoting beverage. It's reported to lower cholesterol, burn body fat, fight arteriosclerosis, strengthen the immune system, and prevent bad breath and gingivitis. It might also protect against cancer, heart disease, and other degenerative diseases.

9. **Think twice about artificial sweeteners.** It's reported they can cause headaches, dizziness, vision problems, sleep disorders, memory loss, fetal brain damage, liver problems, seizures, and the list goes on. I've read that they're especially harmful to children.

10. **Get off your butt!** You already know it but here's a reminder. You have got to move. You don't have to jog ten miles or bench-press anything. Just move. Walk through the mall; play with your kids; run with your dog; bike to the post office; put on some music and dance. No excuses. Just do it.

Bad Snacks vs. Good Snacks

*H*ere are some easy instant changes you can make at home that are sure to improve your health:

INSTEAD OF	SWITCH TO
Margarine for spreading	Butter, in moderation or a spread made with plant sterols
Margarine or butter for sautéing	Olive oil or canola oil
Pretzels	Nuts
Coffee	Tea
Chocolate-covered candies	Dark chocolate–covered peanut clusters
Iceberg lettuce	Romaine lettuce
Creamy salad dressing	Vinaigrette
Candy	Dried fruit
White grapefruit	Pink grapefruit
Cheesecake	Pumpkin pie
Sour cream dip	Bean dip
Microwavable popcorn	Pop your own in canola oil
Green grapes	Red grapes
Bagel	Bran muffin

Why I Drink Green Tea

Green tea has more antioxidants than any other tea, herbal or black, and may be the single most effective element of my daily routine. Every new bit of research provides more and more evidence of the benefits of drinking green tea.

Green tea is just one of the types of tea made from the *Camellia sinensis* plant. They include black tea (Lipton is a black tea), oolong tea, green tea, and the new white tea. These are not herbal teas so they do contain caffeine, although green tea has the least. . . about fifteen milligrams per cup. However, it is also available decaffeinated. The polyphenols in green tea are responsible for its high-antioxidant, free-radical activity, which protects your health and has antiaging properties. It seems like every month I read something new about the benefits of green tea.

The following things have been reported about green tea: It increases metabolism to burn body fat, prevents the absorption of body fat by thirty percent, works with vitamins C and E for optimal benefit, guards smokers' lungs, protects the skin from UV rays, prevents blood clotting and strokes, lowers LDL and raises HDL cholesterol, lowers overall cholesterol and blood pressure, protects against cavities and gingivitis, protects against food poisoning, inhibits the flu virus, prevents bad breath, lowers blood sugar, and strengthens the immune system. It also protects against cancer, heart disease, and many other degenerative diseases, has a calming effect, protects brain cells, aids digestion, and helps you live longer. If even half of these claims are proven to be true, that's good enough for me.

Drinking it before it oxidizes (turns golden) provides the most benefits, so I always make the tea and then cool it down by adding a little cold water so I can drink it sooner. Green tea should be brewed in hot, but not boiling water. Around 170°F is best. I prefer mine unsweetened since it's really mild tasting. There are many different types of green tea and some can taste bitter, so keep trying until you find one you like. It is well worth the effort.

Welcome to My Kitchen

What's in My Pantry?

Here's an inventory of some of the staples in my pantry.

Butter	unsalted
Buttermilk	1%
Canola oil	expeller pressed canola oil
Cheese	reduced fat only
Chocolate chips	mini semisweet chocolate chips
Cocoa	Hershey's and Ghirardelli unsweetened cocoa
Eggs	large size, omega-3 fortified
Flax	Uncle Bob's Ground Flaxseed Meal
Flour	unbleached all-purpose white flour whole-wheat pastry flour
Milk	1% low-fat
Oats	regular rolled oats, not instant
Olive oil	extra virgin olive oil
Peanut butter	Laura Scudders All Natural, Chunky
Rice	converted long-grain white rice, not instant
Syrup	Canadian 100% pure maple syrup

Ten Kitchen Tools I Can't Live Without, Okay. . . Twenty

Tools

1. stand mixer
2. food processor
3. nonstick pots
4. good quality baking pans
5. kitchen scale
6. sifter
7. salad spinner
8. cutting board
9. good set of knives
10. pancake griddle

Gadgets

1. "spoonula" (flexible, spoon-shaped rubber spatula)
2. heat-resistant silicone spatula
3. latex gloves
4. parchment paper
5. waxed paper
6. kitchen timer
7. probe thermometer
8. garlic press
9. nylon whisk
10. Microplane zester

Starting from Scratch to Cook from Scratch

*C*all me a control freak but the more I control what's in my food the better it tastes. And the fewer mystery ingredients there are in my food the better it tastes, so here are some of the things I make for myself:

Bread Crumbs. I have yet to find packaged bread crumbs that don't contain unpronounceable ingredients. So I make my own. I take good quality sandwich bread, remove the crust, cut it into cubes, and dry the cubes on a cookie sheet in the oven at 250°F for about an hour. When they're totally dry and cool, I spin them around in my food processor for about a minute.

TOTAL LABOR INVOLVED: 5 minutes.

Stock. If you read the ingredients on any bouillon cubes or soup mix, you may never buy them again. I make my own stock and cook it down for about 3 hours. Then I strain it and refrigerate overnight. In the morning, all the fat will be on the top and easy to remove. Then I pour my fat-free stock into ice cube trays, freeze, and transfer to a freezer bag to be on the ready.

TOTAL LABOR INVOLVED: 15 minutes to put stock together; 35 seconds to make ice cubes.

Salad Dressing. If people knew how easy it was to make dressing, I think the companies who bottle that gooey, globby stuff would be out of business. Oil and vinegar. End of story.

TOTAL LABOR INVOLVED: 45 seconds or so, depending how close the fridge is.

Apple Sauce. When something is naturally sweet, there's no need to add extra sugar. I just peel and core 2 or 3 apples and cut into chunks. Add just a little water to get started (about 2 tablespoons) then cover in a pot and cook over low heat for about 20 minutes. Then leave it chunky or mash with a fork.

TOTAL LABOR INVOLVED: 5 minutes.

Stewed Prunes. I've never been able to find stewed prunes without a bunch of added sugar, so I put dried prunes in a small pot, barely cover with water, bring to a boil, and simmer for about 10 minutes. Cool and refrigerate with the liquid.

TOTAL LABOR INVOLVED: 2 minutes.

Stuffing Mix. Rather than use store-bought packages of bread cubes loaded with sodium and chemicals, I make my own a few days in advance. Just cube good quality white bread, toss with poultry seasoning (or use fresh herbs later!), and toast on a baking sheet in the oven at 250°F for about an hour or until dry.

TOTAL LABOR INVOLVED: 5 minutes.

My Terms and Techniques Explained

I worked hard to make my recipes easy to follow. Here are a few notes to guide you to recipe success:

- **Read the recipes first.** It's a good idea to read an entire recipe through before starting.

- *Mis en place.* Literally translated this means "put in place." Have all your ingredients in place and ready to use before you start.

- **"Do I Have What It Takes?"** You'll find this information with every recipe. Assuming that we all have regular pots and pans and bowls, it's to alert you to a specific tool or cookware that is vital to the recipe.

- **"Shopping List."** The shopping list included with each recipe is written in the same order in which the items appear in the recipe. It includes every single ingredient you will need to make that particular dish.

- **Pans.** All the pans I use are nonstick.

    Sauté Pan. A pan that is flat on the bottom with high perpendicular sides, usually about two inches high. These pans almost always have lids.

    Fry Pan. A pan where the edge curves or slopes up slightly so you can tilt and slide ingredients out.

- **Size does matter.** Using the wrong size baking pan can cause cake failure. Try to use the exact size specified.

- **Measuring flour.** The method I use is to stir the flour in the canister first to aerate it, and then scoop it with a measuring cup. Without tapping or shaking the cup, I level the top with the back of a knife.

- **Measuring sugar.** I just dip the measuring cup in the canister then level it off with the back of a knife, no tapping or shaking.

- **Eggs.** For all my cooking and baking I only use large eggs. I prefer eggs fortified with omega-3 and vitamin E.

- **Butter.** I only use unsalted butter. That way if the recipe calls for $1/4$ teaspoon of salt, that's all I'm getting. Plus, I think unsalted butter tastes better.

- **Baking pans.** You'll get the best baking result using shiny aluminum pans and not dark ones. Most nonsticks are dark and retain more heat and can burn cookies or dry out edges of a cake.

- **Greasing pans.** It's easy to grease pans with that spray stuff, but I can't stand the smell of it or the feel of it. When a pan needs greasing I use butter or my butter-and-canola oil mixture (see page 48) that I always keep in the fridge.

- **Cakes.** For cakes that are flat on top and don't mound, try using a cake strip. They also help prevent the edges from drying out. They are available at kitchenware stores. You saturate them in water and then wrap them around the cake pan before baking. I always use them for my cakes.

- **Storing muffins.** Muffins are best eaten while still warm or within a few hours. Once they're wrapped in plastic and refrigerated they become rubbery so I recommend freezing them instead. Reheat frozen muffins in the microwave for thirty seconds or thaw at room temperature for one hour.

- **Waxed paper.** You can save a lot of cleanup by measuring dry ingredients onto waxed paper instead of in a bowl. Just lift both sides of the paper and pour. Then toss the waxed paper. (Parchment works too, but waxed paper is cheaper.)

Recipe Disaster? Questions? Suggestions?

Just go to **www.jennyjones.com** and check out the *Look Good, Feel Great Cookbook* section. You will find updates on these recipes, a place to ask questions, as well as new recipes and food talk.

My Favorite Breakfasts

(apple)

Blueberry Pancakes   MAKES 6 TO 8 PANCAKES

Pancakes from scratch are so easy to make there is no need to buy a packaged mix. If you can't afford a down payment on fresh blueberries you can substitute other fruits like chopped apples or bananas, or even use frozen berries. Just rinse frozen berries and pat them dry, then sprinkle them on the pancakes while they're cooking but before you flip them over. I make pancakes every weekend, so I bought a nonstick electric griddle (no greasing necessary), and now I can make all the pancakes at once so they can be served hot. If your griddle is smaller, you can cook them in smaller batches and keep them warm in a 200°F oven. The secret to fluffy pancakes is not to overmix.

I cup all-purpose flour

I teaspoon baking powder

$^1/_2$ teaspoon baking soda

Pinch of salt

I cup low-fat buttermilk

I large egg

2 tablespoons canola oil

I cup fresh blueberries, washed and patted dry

Start-to-Finish
20 minutes

Do I Have What It Takes?
You'll need a nonstick pancake griddle or a large nonstick pan.

Shopping List
all-purpose flour ▪ baking powder ▪ baking soda ▪ buttermilk ▪ egg ▪ canola oil ▪ blueberries

1. Preheat a nonstick electric griddle to 375°F or a large nonstick skillet on the stove over medium-high heat.

2. In a large bowl sift together the flour, baking powder, baking soda, and salt. In another bowl, or right in the measuring cup, whisk together the buttermilk, egg, and oil.

3. Make a well in the flour mixture and pour in the buttermilk mixture all at once. Gently stir together until barely moistened and still lumpy. Do not beat. Gently fold in the blueberries. A spatula or a "spoonula" is great for all this mixing.

4. Using about $^1/_4$ cup of batter for each pancake, pour onto the ungreased griddle, leaving room for them to spread. Cook until tiny bubbles form on top and the edges are dry, about 3 minutes, and then turn once and cook for another 3 minutes. Serve hot.

Health Benefits

Blueberries are the new antiaging heroes. They are sometimes called "brain food" because they can help your memory, and protect against Alzheimer's and senility. They may protect against cardiovascular disease, cancer, diabetes, macular degeneration, and cataracts. They can also strengthen your immune system, urinary tract, and bones as well as improve your skin.

I picked up this pretty turquoise plate specifically for my blueberry pancake photo, and the cloth was from the remnants section of a fabric store.

I had to work fast on this picture to avoid having too much syrup on the plate. Luckily, the first few shots worked and resulted in one of my favorite photos in this book.

Apple Brancakes MAKES 6 TO 8 PANCAKES

These are so good they don't even need syrup. You can find unprocessed wheat bran at the health food store, sometimes called Miller's bran. I like Granny Smith apples for pancakes but you can also use Gala or another tart apple. You'll need one medium apple. A nonstick griddle is best because you don't need to grease it with oil or butter, just drop the cakes right on it. The secret to fluffy pancakes is not to overmix . . . no electric beaters, for sure. Stir by hand, just until it's all incorporated and use the batter right away or let it stand for up to 30 minutes. A "spoonula" works great for stirring pancake batter.

$^2/_3$ cup all-purpose flour

$^1/_3$ cup whole-grain pastry flour

2 teaspoons sugar

$1^1/_2$ teaspoons baking powder

$^1/_2$ teaspoon baking soda

$^1/_8$ teaspoon salt

$^1/_4$ cup wheat bran

$1^1/_4$ cups low-fat buttermilk

1 large egg

1 tablespoon canola oil

1 cup peeled and cored, finely diced apple (about $^1/_4$ -inch dice)

Start-to-Finish
15 minutes

Do I Have What It Takes?
You'll need a nonstick pancake griddle or a large non-stick skillet.

1 Preheat a nonstick griddle to 375°F or preheat a large non-stick skillet over medium-high heat.

2 In a large bowl, sift together the all-purpose flour, whole-grain flour, sugar, baking powder, baking soda, and salt. Stir in the wheat bran.

3 In another bowl, whisk together the buttermilk, egg, and oil. Add the buttermilk mixture to the flour mixture all at once, stirring just until moistened. The batter should be lumpy. Gently fold in the apples.

4 Pour about $^1/_4$ cup of batter per pancake onto the griddle and cook for about 3 minutes. Turn once after bubbles appear on the top and cook another 2 to 3 minutes. Serve hot.

Health Benefits

Fiber is the winner here, which is key to a healthy colon. Besides fiber, apples also contain pectin, which lowers cholesterol, and may protect against blood clots and cancer.

Shopping List
all-purpose flour ▪ whole-grain pastry flour ▪ sugar ▪ baking powder ▪ baking soda ▪ wheat bran ▪ buttermilk ▪ egg ▪ canola oil ▪ apple

This may look like an easy picture to get... just pancakes on a plate, right?

Not so, my friends. To get the butter melting just so, dripping down just so,

was quite an accomplishment for me especially since I only had about three minutes

before the butter was all gone.

Scrambled Eggs that Rock

MAKES 2 SERVINGS

This is one of my favorite breakfasts. It's a complete meal with a lot of nutritional goodness. Chop the vegetables in fairly big chunks so they stay firm. You can use any color (or mixture) of bell peppers, and for the chile I used a mild Anaheim pepper but you can use a hotter one like jalapeño. The best potato would be a red skin, new potato, or Yukon gold. You can steam, boil, or bake them in advance, unless you have some left over. Whenever I boil potatoes for potato salad I throw in a couple of extra ones to save just so I can make this breakfast. My mother always kept boiled potatoes in the fridge and would eat them as a snack with a little mayo. Actually, it was a lot of mayo.

1 medium potato

1 teaspoon unsalted butter

1 teaspoon canola oil

1 cup coarsely chopped onion (1 small onion)

1 cup coarsely chopped red bell pepper

$1/4$ cup thick-sliced chile pepper (see Headnote)

4 large eggs

2 tablespoons 1% low-fat milk

$1/2$ teaspoon salt

Black pepper to taste

Start-to-Finish
20 minutes

Do I Have What It Takes?
No special equipment is needed.

1   Scrub the potato or peel if desired. Cut it into 1-inch chunks and steam or boil for about 5 minutes. Set aside.

2   In a large skillet over medium heat, add the butter and oil. Add the onion and cook, stirring, until golden and translucent, 2 to 3 minutes. Add the cooked potato, bell pepper, and chile pepper and cook, stirring, until the potatoes are nicely browned, about 5 minutes.

3   While the vegetables are cooking, in a small bowl combine the eggs, milk, salt, and pepper.

4   Reduce the heat to low and push the vegetable mixture to one side of the skillet. Add the egg mixture and cook separately for 1 minute. Stir in the vegetables and cook until the eggs are done, 1 to 2 minutes more.

Kitchen Tip

How to Tell a Hard-Boiled Egg from a Raw One

Spin the egg on a table. The hard-boiled egg will spin quickly, but the raw one will wobble slowly.

Health Benefits

Eggs are an excellent source of protein, which supports everything from your brain, muscles, heart, and blood, right down to your hair, nails, and skin. Onions can protect you from cancer, heart disease, stroke, and memory loss, as well as help fight infection. The peppers can also protect against heart disease and cancer as well as memory loss and macular degeneration. Peppers are reported to slow the aging process and strengthen the urinary tract and immune system. They help to burn fat.

I chose a minimalist style for this photo with my own dinner plate from home and a fork from an antique mall in Sherman Oaks, California. The nicely browned potatoes just prove that you can brown foods in a nonstick pan.

Whole-Grain Waffles with Berries

MAKES ABOUT 6 WAFFLES

Not all whole-grain pastry flours are the same, so look for one that has a fine grain. And not all waffle makers are the same, so adjust the amount of batter you use for each waffle accordingly. I'm not a big fan of cooking sprays but if you need to grease your waffle maker, it makes the job easy. Here is how I eat my three waffles: First waffle—real maple syrup. Second waffle—a mountain of berries on top. Third waffle—a scoop of low-fat vanilla yogurt and a mountain of berries on top. After the third waffle, I go for a walk.

1¼ cups whole-grain pastry flour

1½ teaspoons baking powder

½ teaspoon baking soda

⅛ teaspoon salt

2 large eggs, separated

1 cup low-fat buttermilk

2 tablespoons canola oil

½ cup sliced raw almonds (optional)

2 cups fresh berries

Start-to-Finish
20 minutes

Do I Have What It Takes?
You'll need an electric waffle maker—they make great Christmas presents.

1   Preheat a waffle maker and grease it with cooking spray, if necessary.

2   Into a large bowl, sift the flour, baking powder, baking soda, and salt.

3   In a small bowl, beat the egg whites with an electric hand mixer until they hold stiff peaks, reserving the egg yolks.

4   In a small bowl or measuring cup, combine the buttermilk, oil, and egg yolks and gently stir it into the flour mixture until just combined, stirring by hand. Gently fold in the egg whites. If a few lumps of egg white remain that's okay; just don't overmix and no electric mixers, please!

5   Pour about ½ cup of batter per waffle on your preheated grids, and quickly top each one with 1½ tablespoons of sliced almonds. Close the lid and bake until the steaming stops, about 5 minutes. Do not open the lid until they're done. Serve with fresh berries.

Health Benefits

Whole-grain flour provides fiber to help prevent constipation. Fiber can also help with weight loss and may protect you from heart disease, colon cancer, diverticulitis, and stroke. Almonds provide heart-healthy fat that is believed to protect against heart disease and diabetes. Berries may help fight cancer, heart and eye disease, urinary tract infection, and memory loss. Berries may also boost your immune system and help prevent diabetes, senility, and Alzheimer's. Blueberries have also been called brain food.

Shopping List
whole-grain pastry flour ▪ baking powder ▪ baking soda ▪ eggs ▪ buttermilk ▪ canola oil ▪ sliced almonds ▪ fresh berries

Blueberries always look dusty but I swear I washed and patted them dry. These are all discount store dishes with a yard of fabric for my tablecloth. After I placed the raspberries, I realized that with the two colors of berries this breakfast could also serve as a quick game of tic-tac-toe.

Four-Grain Pancakes

Whole grains and fiber are vital to good health and here's a great way to eat them. Heck, you can call these Five-Grain Pancakes by mixing some rye flour in with the buckwheat, as long as it totals $1/4$ cup. If you use a nonstick pan you won't need any butter or oil for greasing. I cook all my pancakes on a dry, nonstick griddle. If yours is not nonstick just rub a stick of butter over it for a light greasing. I find that having six or eight pancakes on the griddle makes it cool down quickly, which is why I raise the temperature as soon as I pour the batter. This maintains the initial temperature for faster cooking.

$1/2$ cup whole-grain pastry flour

$1/2$ cup regular rolled oats, not instant

$1/4$ cup buckwheat flour

$1/4$ cup stone-ground yellow cornmeal

1 tablespoon sugar

$1 1/2$ teaspoons baking powder

$1/2$ teaspoon baking soda

$1/8$ teaspoon salt

$1 1/2$ cups low-fat buttermilk

1 large egg

2 tablespoons canola oil

Start-to-Finish
30 minutes

Do I Have What It Takes?
You'll need a pancake griddle or a large skillet.

1 Preheat a nonstick electric griddle to 375°F or a large nonstick skillet on the stove over medium-high heat.

2 In a large bowl, combine the whole-grain pastry flour, oats, buckwheat flour, cornmeal, sugar, baking powder, baking soda, and salt. Stir well to combine evenly.

3 In a smaller bowl, whisk together the buttermilk, egg, and oil. Add the buttermilk mixture to the flour mixture all at once, gently stirring until well blended. Let stand for 5 minutes to soften the grains.

4 Pour about $1/3$ cup batter per pancake onto the hot griddle. Raise the griddle temperature to 400°F, or the stove temperature up a little higher and cook for about 2 minutes per side, turning once when the pancakes have little bubbles on the top and the edges are dry. Serve hot with maple syrup or honey.

Health Benefits

Oats keep your cholesterol and blood sugar in check and may also protect your immune system, bones, and heart. Whole grains can help prevent obesity, diabetes, high blood pressure, heart disease, and cancer.

Shopping List
whole-grain pastry flour ▪ oats ▪ buckwheat flour ▪ stone-ground yellow cornmeal ▪ sugar ▪ baking powder ▪ baking soda ▪ buttermilk ▪ egg ▪ canola oil

I found this beaded place mat at a T.J. Maxx store in the suburbs of Chicago, and the breakfast plate at Ace Hardware. These pancakes may look overdone but they're not. Whole grain always looks darker.

Superfood Scramble

I've never been good at omelettes but I can scramble eggs like a big girl. There are tons of things you can mix into scrambled eggs, such as red pepper, broccoli, asparagus, greens, steak, ham, salmon, tomatoes, etc., but spinach is just about the ultimate superfood. Of course you can use 2 eggs and 3 or 4 whites, or even all egg whites. Mushrooms are better wiped or brushed clean rather than washed.

4 large eggs

2 tablespoons 1% low-fat milk

$1/4$ teaspoon salt

Black pepper to taste

1 teaspoon unsalted butter

$1/4$ cup diced onion

1 cup sliced mushrooms ($1/8$ inch thick)

Half of a 6-ounce bag of baby spinach

Start-to-Finish
20 minutes

Do I Have What It Takes?
No special equipment is needed.

Shopping List
eggs ▪ milk ▪ unsalted butter ▪ onion ▪ mushrooms ▪ spinach

1 In a small bowl, combine the eggs, milk, salt, and pepper. Set aside.

2 In a large pan over medium heat, melt the butter. Add the onion and cook, stirring, for about 1 minute. Add the mushrooms and cook, stirring, until the mushrooms are soft, about 2 minutes. Add the spinach and cook, stirring, just until the spinach is wilted, about 2 minutes longer.

3 Remove the pan from the heat and push the spinach mixture to one side of the pan. Pour in the egg mixture, stir, and cook for a minute. Stir everything together and continue cooking until the eggs are done, about 2 minutes. Finish over low heat if the eggs aren't cooked through.

Kitchen Tip

For Perfect Hard-Boiled Eggs

Put eggs into a saucepan and cover with cold water. Bring to a full boil, then remove from heat and cover. Let stand for 17 minutes. Drain and run cold water over the eggs for a minute to make them easier to peel. That's it. No green stuff around the yolk. Perfect hard-boiled eggs every time.

Health Benefits

Spinach does so much: It can protect your eyes from cataracts and macular degeneration and the rest of you from heart disease, stroke, and cancer. It may also prevent birth defects, osteoporosis, and aging of the brain and is even good for your skin. Mushrooms are reported to boost the immune system.

Boy did this smell good while I was taking the picture. My tablecloth is some leftover fabric from a pillow I made and the plate was a "second" I found on sale. And if you look throughout this book you'll find that same fork in about eight different pictures.

Dutch Baby
MAKES 2 SERVINGS

Here's a fantastic way to add fresh fruit to your breakfast. You can serve this beautiful wavy pancake with just about any fruit—strawberries, blueberries, peaches, raspberries, bananas, papaya, mangoes, pineapples, or whatever is in season. Now here's the thing: Everyone should be seated and ready with a bowl of fresh fruit when the pancake is done because it doesn't stay poofy for long. And be careful handling the very hot pan... it's easy to forget and grab the handle with your bare hand. The batter can be made ahead and refrigerated. To dust it with powdered sugar just put the sugar in a sifter or sieve and lightly tap over the pancake.

1 cup 1% low-fat milk

3 large eggs

2 tablespoons sugar

$1/4$ teaspoon salt

Pinch of nutmeg

1 cup all-purpose flour

1 teaspoon unsalted butter, for greasing pan

1 tablespoon powdered sugar, for garnish

Fresh fruit, for serving (see Headnote)

Start-to-Finish:
Once the oven is preheated, 20 minutes

Do I Have What It Takes?
You'll need a 10-inch cast-iron skillet and a thick oven mitt.

1. Place a 10-inch cast-iron skillet in the oven and preheat the oven to 425°F.

2. In a medium bowl, whisk together the milk, eggs, sugar, salt, and nutmeg until well blended. Add the flour and whisk until well blended and smooth, about 30 seconds.

3. Carefully remove the hot pan from the oven and swirl the butter around the inside, then quickly add the batter. Return immediately to the oven and bake for about 15 minutes, or until the edges are golden.

4. Carefully slide the pancake onto a large serving plate, lifting the edges with a metal spatula. Dust with powdered sugar, cut into wedges, serve immediately, and top with fruit at the table.

Health Benefits

As pictured (with blueberries, raspberries, papaya, and banana), the benefits are huge. With raspberries and blueberries you may get protection against cardiovascular disease, cancer, diabetes, senility, macular degeneration, cataracts, and Alzheimer's, as well as a healthier urinary tract and improved skin. Choose papaya and you could lower your blood pressure and cholesterol as well as ease your arthritis, bronchitis, and asthma. Bananas are good defenders against hypertension, high cholesterol, and heart disease.

Shopping List
milk ▪ eggs ▪ sugar ▪ nutmeg ▪ flour ▪ unsalted butter ▪ powdered sugar ▪ fresh fruit (banana, blueberries, raspberries, papaya)

Lights! Camera! Potholders! These poofy pancakes lose some of their poof quickly, so I literally ran with it to my photo table to immediately grab a picture. I had to get it right the first time because after about two minutes, it was flat as a . . . well, you know.

Extreme Oatmeal MAKES 2 SERVINGS

Got five minutes? That's about all it takes to lower your cholesterol. If you're tired of the instant one-minute Spackle disguised as oatmeal, then try this easy and oh-so-nutritious breakfast. It's great with added milk, brown sugar, or fruit like bananas or berries. When cooking oatmeal I recommend not abandoning your post. Stay at the stove because if it spills over it makes a big mess, and eating breakfast while under stress is not recommended.

2 cups water

Pinch of salt

1 cup regular oats, not instant

$1/3$ cup oat bran

Start-to-Finish
7 minutes

Do I Have What It Takes?
A saucepan is all you need.

Shopping List
oats ▪ oat bran

1   In a medium saucepan, bring the water and salt to a boil.

2   Stir in the oats and oat bran and once the mixture boils, reduce the heat to low. Cook uncovered, stirring regularly, for about 5 minutes.

Health Benefits

Oats, and especially oat bran, are proven to lower cholesterol and stabilize blood sugar, and are recommended for diabetics. Oats may also help protect against colon cancer and heart disease and the fiber can help with weight loss.

Muffins and Quick Breads

Sweet Raspberry-Corn Muffins
MAKES 12 MUFFINS

These beautifully colored gold and crimson delights can be part of a breakfast, a mid-morning snack, or how about with company for an afternoon tea? Fresh raspberries seem to be available almost year-round but the prices can be steep. I always look over my raspberries, before making the investment. Right there in the produce section, I open up the plastic lid that they don't want you to see through. Don't buy fresh raspberries without eyeballing them first, inside and out.

1³/₄ cups all-purpose flour

1 cup stone-ground yellow cornmeal

³/₄ cup plus 1 tablespoon sugar

1 tablespoon baking powder

¹/₄ teaspoon salt

1 cup 1% low-fat milk

³/₄ cup canola oil

2 large eggs

1 cup raspberries, washed and drained on paper towels

1 tablespoon sugar, for sprinkling

Start-to-Finish
35 minutes

Do I Have What It Takes?
You'll need a 12-cup muffin pan, preferably nonstick.

1   Preheat the oven to 400°F and lightly grease a 12-cup muffin pan with butter.

2   Into a large bowl, sift together the flour, cornmeal, sugar, baking powder, and salt.

3   In another bowl, combine the milk, oil, and eggs. Pour the milk mixture into the flour mixture all at once. Using a spatula or a "spoonula" combine just until the flour mixture is moistened. Gently fold in the raspberries, being careful not to smash them. Do not overmix.

4   Divide the batter into the muffin cups and sprinkle each one with sugar. Bake for 20 minutes or until the edges are golden. Immediately remove the muffins from the pan to a wire cooling rack. Serve warm.

Health Benefits

Raspberries contain beneficial fiber, good for diabetics and for warding off heart disease. They may also protect against cancer and memory loss as well as protect your urinary tract and immune system. Cornmeal is believed to protect against macular degeneration and cancer and also supports the immune system.

Shopping List
flour ▪ cornmeal ▪ sugar ▪ baking powder ▪ milk ▪ canola oil ▪ eggs ▪ fresh raspberries

This pretty plate was discovered at an antique shop, and I found the antique butter knife the same day. The pink glass came from a shop in Redding, California, and the beautiful hand-crocheted tablecloth was a gift from my friend Lynda Frangos in Canada.

Oatmeal Banana Muffins MAKES 12 MUFFINS

These filling muffins make a nice midday snack when you want something a little sweet. You'll need 2 ripe bananas for this recipe and the riper the bananas, the sweeter. You can even add some crushed dried banana chips for extra crunch.

WALNUT TOPPING

1 tablespoon melted unsalted butter

1 tablespoon light brown sugar

$^1/_2$ cup finely chopped walnuts

MUFFIN BATTER

2 cups all-purpose flour

$^2/_3$ cup sugar

2 teaspoons baking powder

$^1/_2$ teaspoon baking soda

$^1/_4$ teaspoon salt

1$^1/_2$ cups regular rolled oats (not instant)

1 cup 1% low-fat milk

$^1/_2$ cup canola oil

2 large eggs

1 teaspoon vanilla extract

$^1/_2$ cup mashed banana (1 medium banana)

$^1/_2$ cup finely chopped walnuts

$^2/_3$ cup diced banana (1 large banana)

1. Preheat the oven to 375°F. Lightly grease a 12-cup muffin pan with butter.

2. For the Walnut Topping, in a small bowl, combine the melted butter, brown sugar, and $^1/_2$ cup chopped walnuts and set aside.

3. In a large bowl, sift together the flour, sugar, baking powder, baking soda, and salt. Stir in the oats.

4. In another bowl using an electric mixer on medium speed, combine the milk, oil, eggs, vanilla, and mashed banana until there are no lumps. Make a well in the flour mixture and add the banana mixture all at once. Using a spatula or large spoon, stir gently until just barely combined. Fold in the $^1/_2$ cup chopped walnuts and diced banana. The batter should be a little lumpy, so don't overmix.

5. Divide the batter equally into the 12 muffin cups and, using your fingers, sprinkle each muffin with the walnut topping. Bake for 25 minutes or until lightly browned.

6. Immediately remove the muffins from the pan to a wire cooling rack.

Health Benefits

Oatmeal has been proven to lower cholesterol and stabilize blood sugar. It may also help prevent diabetes, diverticulitis, heart disease, osteoporosis, colon cancer, and bone loss. Oats and nuts keep you full longer to help control weight. Walnuts and bananas also protect your heart and can lower your blood pressure as well as support your immune system. Walnuts are the best nuts to eat for lowering cholesterol.

Start-to-Finish
45 minutes

Do I Have What It Takes?
You'll need a 12-cup muffin pan, preferably nonstick.

Shopping List
unsalted butter ▪ brown sugar ▪ walnuts ▪ flour ▪ sugar ▪ baking powder ▪ baking soda ▪ oats ▪ milk ▪ canola oil ▪ eggs ▪ vanilla extract ▪ bananas

I didn't have to work too hard to set this shot. I always cool muffins on a metal rack so all I had to do was get my camera. I debated on whether to pick up the pieces of walnuts that rolled off and decided to leave them there because in reality, some of them will fall off.

Apple Breakfast Bread MAKES I LOAF

Don't be misled by the name here. This tasty bread is not intended to BE breakfast but to have WITH a healthy breakfast, like maybe a hard-boiled egg with whole-grain toast and then a slice of apple bread with green tea. It's also perfect for a midmorning snack or even dessert after dinner. The point is if you're going to eat sweet bread, have one with beneficial fruit in it. You don't have to use the parchment paper liner but it does make for easy removal after baking.

TOPPING

1 tablespoon sugar

$1/4$ teaspoon cinnamon

BREAD

$2^1/2$ cups all-purpose flour

$1/2$ cup sugar

$2^1/2$ teaspoons baking powder

$1/2$ teaspoon baking soda

$1/4$ teaspoon cinnamon

$1/4$ teaspoon salt

1 cup low-fat buttermilk

$1/4$ cup canola oil

2 large eggs

$1/2$ teaspoon vanilla extract

2 small Granny Smith apples

Start-to-Finish
1 hour and 20 minutes, mostly unattended

Do I Have What It Takes?
You'll need a 9 x 5-inch loaf pan, preferably nonstick.

1 Preheat the oven to 325°F. Grease a 9 x 5-inch loaf pan with butter and insert parchment paper across the long sides and extending down a few inches.

2 For the topping, in a tiny bowl combine the 1 tablespoon sugar and $1/4$ teaspoon cinnamon and set aside.

3 Into a large bowl, sift together the flour, $1/2$ cup sugar, baking powder, baking soda, $1/4$ teaspoon cinnamon, and salt.

4 In a smaller bowl, or right in the measuring cup, whisk together the buttermilk, oil, eggs, and vanilla.

5 Peel 1 apple and dice into $1/2$-inch pieces to make 1 cup. Peel and quarter second apple and slice into about twenty-four $1/4$-inch slices.

6 Make a well in the flour mixture and pour in the buttermilk mixture all at once. Using a large spatula gently fold ingredients together. When they are almost combined add the diced apples. Do not overmix.

7 Spoon the batter into the loaf pan and smooth the top with a spatula. Push apple slices half way down into the batter, working down the length of the loaf. Sprinkle with the topping mixture.

8　Bake for 50 to 60 minutes or until a toothpick inserted in center of loaf comes out clean. Cool in the pan for 15 minutes, then remove to a wire cooling rack.

Health Benefits

Apples provide fiber, which is important for a healthy colon. They may also provide some protection against cancer, heart disease, diabetes, and stroke.

Shopping List
sugar ▪ cinnamon ▪
flour ▪ baking powder ▪
baking soda ▪ buttermilk ▪
canola oil ▪ eggs ▪
vanilla extract ▪
Granny Smith apples

This photo started with a piece of polka-dot cotton from the fabric store. Two weeks later I found the fabulous antique cup and saucer and just knew it would match. Then I polished up an old cake server to capture the reflection of the tea cup. I sliced the bread just right so you could see the slices of apple.

Blueberry Muffins MAKES 12 MUFFINS

I can't think of anything better to do when fresh blueberries are in season than make blueberry muffins. Be sure to examine the blueberries carefully for any bad or moldy ones. I do this by spreading the berries on a paper towel, and then I wash and pat them dry. Any muffins that don't get eaten within hours are better frozen; they can be thawed in about an hour at room temperature or in 30 seconds in the microwave.

$2^{1}/_{2}$ cups all-purpose flour

$^{1}/_{2}$ cup sugar

$2^{1}/_{2}$ teaspoons baking powder

$^{1}/_{2}$ teaspoon baking soda

$^{1}/_{8}$ teaspoon salt

1 cup low-fat buttermilk

$^{1}/_{3}$ cup canola oil

2 large eggs

$^{1}/_{2}$ teaspoon vanilla extract

1 heaping cup fresh blueberries, washed and patted dry

2 teaspoons sugar for sprinkling

Start-to-Finish
30 minutes

Do I Have What It Takes?
You'll need a 12-cup muffin pan, preferably nonstick.

Shopping List
flour ▪ sugar ▪ baking powder ▪ baking soda ▪ buttermilk ▪ canola oil ▪ eggs ▪ vanilla extract ▪ fresh blueberries

1   Preheat the oven to 400°F. Lightly grease a 12-cup muffin pan with butter.

2   Into a large bowl, sift together the flour, $^{1}/_{2}$ cup sugar, baking powder, baking soda, and salt.

3   In another bowl or in a measuring cup, whisk together the buttermilk, oil, eggs, and vanilla. Make a well in the flour mixture and add the buttermilk mixture all at once. Gently fold them together with a spatula, adding the blueberries at the end. The batter should be a bit lumpy, so don't overmix.

4   Evenly divide the batter between 12 muffin cups and lightly sprinkle each one with sugar. Bake for about 20 minutes or until the tops are golden. Immediately remove the muffins from the pan to a wire cooling rack.

Health Benefits

Eat those blueberries! These immune-strengthening berries are reported to protect against cardiovascular disease, cancer, diabetes, senility, macular degeneration, cataracts, osteoporosis, Alzheimer's, and birth defects. They are considered "brain food" and may also protect your urinary tract and improve your skin.

The pink plate came from a home store in Barrington, Illinois. The golden

brown tops on these muffins result from sprinkling some sugar on top before baking.

I always eat the bottom half first and save the crunchy top for dessert.

Banana Walnut Bread MAKES 1 LOAF

I wanted to call this Banana Flax Bread but you might not be reading this if I did. It's really a delicious, moist, sweet bread, and the flax is just a bonus. The bananas should be very ripe—that's when they're the sweetest. It'll be much easier to remove this loaf from the pan when it's done if you line the greased pan with parchment paper, leaving an inch at each long side for your "handles." I like this best served cold with a cup of green tea. Make sure you use ground flaxseed meal because the whole seed will not digest well.

2 cups all-purpose flour

1/2 cup sugar

2 teaspoons baking powder

1 teaspoon baking soda

1/4 teaspoon salt

1/2 cup ground flaxseed meal

1/3 cup canola oil

2 large eggs

1 cup mashed bananas
  (2 large bananas)

1/3 cup 1% low-fat milk

1/2 teaspoon vanilla extract

2/3 cup diced walnuts

Start-to-Finish
1 hour and 15 minutes, mostly unattended

Do I Have What It Takes?
You'll need a 9 x 5-inch loaf pan, preferably nonstick.

1 Preheat the oven to 350°F and lightly grease a 9 x 5-inch loaf pan with butter. Line with parchment paper if desired, leaving extra on the long sides for lifting finished bread from the pan.

2 Into a large bowl, sift together the flour, sugar, baking powder, baking soda, and salt. Stir in the flaxseed meal.

3 In another bowl using an electric mixer, beat the oil, eggs, bananas, milk, and vanilla until well blended and smooth, about 1 minute. Add the banana mixture to the flour mixture and combine with a spoon or spatula, adding the walnuts at the end. Do not overmix.

4 Spoon the batter into the prepared loaf pan and bake for 1 hour or until a toothpick inserted into the center comes out clean. Cool on a rack in the pan for 5 minutes, then remove from pan to cool completely.

Health Benefits

Bananas can lower your cholesterol and blood pressure, and prevent hypertension, diabetes, and heart disease. The flaxseed meal and walnuts both provide important omega-3 fatty acids which can protect you from coronary artery disease; diabetes; high blood pressure; breast, colon, and prostate cancers; hypertension; arthritis; lupus; constipation; vision loss; and even depression. Omega-3s can also boost your immune system and even give you shiny hair, good skin, and strong nails.

Shopping List
flour ▪ sugar ▪ baking powder ▪ baking soda ▪ ground flaxseed meal ▪ canola oil ▪ eggs ▪ bananas ▪ milk ▪ vanilla extract ▪ walnuts

This beautiful cake stand came from a discount store and the fabric was purchased by the yard. I love the combination of these two colors together.

It was late in the afternoon and with the sun being low it showed off the turquoise plate

beautifully. Banana bread should be cut thick like this so it doesn't fall apart.

Pumpkin Chocolate Chip Muffins
MAKES 12 MUFFINS

I've never met anyone who doesn't love these muffins. You can substitute lots of other things for the chocolate chips, like all walnuts, pecans, raisins, cranberries, or just make them plain. If you don't have whole-grain pastry flour, you can use 2$^1/_2$ cups of all-purpose flour, but the whole-grain flour provides extra fiber. The secret to good muffins is not to overmix. Muffins don't keep very well so I freeze them as soon as they cool and it only takes about 30 seconds to microwave one. Sometimes I put a frozen one in my purse and by the time I'm ready for it, it's ready for me.

2 cups all-purpose flour

$^1/_2$ cup whole-grain pastry flour

$^1/_2$ cup sugar

2 teaspoons baking powder

1 teaspoon cinnamon

1 teaspoon nutmeg

$^1/_4$ teaspoon salt

1 cup canned pumpkin

1 cup 1% low-fat milk

$^1/_3$ cup canola oil

2 large eggs

$^1/_3$ cup mini semisweet chocolate chips

$^1/_2$ cup chopped walnuts

Start-to-Finish
40 minutes

Do I Have What It Takes?
You'll need a 12-cup muffin pan, preferably nonstick.

1   Preheat the oven to 400°F. Lightly grease a 12-cup muffin pan. I use butter to grease my pans because it seems to work best and it's real food, unlike the cooking sprays.

2   Into a large bowl, sift together the all-purpose flour, whole-grain pastry flour, sugar, baking powder, cinnamon, nutmeg, and salt. In another bowl, combine the pumpkin, milk, oil, and eggs. An electric mixer handles this well, but a whisk or fork will get it done, too.

3   Make a well in the flour mixture and add the pumpkin mixture all at once, stirring with a spatula just until the flour is moistened. A few bits of visible flour are okay at this point. Gently fold in the chocolate chips and nuts. Do not overmix.

4   Divide the batter between the muffin cups and bake for 20 to 25 minutes. You can test for doneness by inserting a toothpick into a muffin. If it comes out clean, they're done. Remove the muffins from the pan right away to a cooling rack.

Health Benefits

Pumpkin supports the immune system as well as lung and heart health and may protect against macular degeneration and certain cancers. Walnuts can lower cholesterol and protect against heart disease, arthritis, hypertension, and macular degeneration. Both pumpkin and walnuts are also good for the hair, nails, and skin.

Shopping List
all-purpose flour ▪ whole-grain pastry flour ▪ sugar ▪ baking powder ▪ cinnamon ▪ nutmeg ▪ canned pumpkin ▪ milk ▪ canola oil ▪ eggs ▪ mini chocolate chips ▪ walnuts

Wasn't there a movie called Attack of the 50-Foot Muffin? Maybe not. I wanted you to smell the chocolate chips so I zoomed in very close on this photo. The cup and saucer came from Pier One. I had to keep replacing the muffin in this photo because the heat from the lights kept melting the chocolate chips.

Jalapeño Corn Bread MAKES 8 SERVINGS

Be careful working with jalapeños! I recommend using rubber or latex gloves to remove the seeds because if you don't . . . and then you touch your eye . . . ouch! How easy is this recipe? Just mix it all up in one big bowl. Try to avoid preshredded cheese and grate your own for a moister bread. The best corn bread is made in a cast-iron skillet that's preheated and sizzles when you add the batter. If you don't have one you can use a greased 9-inch round baking pan, but don't preheat the pan and raise the oven temperature to 400°F. This bread is great served hot but I love to snack on it cold.

2 ears fresh corn (to make about 2 cups kernels)

1/2 of a small onion, grated (about 1/2 cup)

2 ounces reduced-fat cheddar cheese, grated

2 jalapeño peppers, diced (about 1/3 cup)

1 cup stone-ground yellow cornmeal

1/2 cup all-purpose flour

2 teaspoons baking powder

1/2 teaspoon baking soda

1/2 teaspoon salt

1 cup low-fat buttermilk

1/3 cup canola oil

2 large eggs

2 tablespoons sugar

Start-to-Finish
45 minutes

Do I Have What It Takes?
You'll need a 9- or 10-inch cast-iron skillet, a hand or box grater, and a thick oven mitt.

1 Place a 9- or 10-inch cast iron skillet in the oven and preheat to 375°F.

2 Into a large tall bowl using a sharp knife, cut the corn off the cob, then scrape the cob with the dull side of the knife to get lots of nice thick corn juice. Shred the onion and cheese on the same grater, right into the bowl. Add the jalapeños, cornmeal, flour, baking powder, baking soda, salt, buttermilk, canola oil, eggs, and sugar and combine well.

3 Lightly coat the hot skillet with oil (use a thick oven mitt!). I just pour a tablespoon of oil into the pan then quickly swish it around with a paper towel held by a pair of tongs. Immediately pour the batter into the hot skillet and return to the oven. Bake for about 30 minutes, until golden.

Kitchen Tip
To Cut Down on Saturated Fat

Instead of using butter, which I love, I mix it half and half with canola oil, which is monounsaturated and actually good for your heart. I use this mixture in place of butter on toast, pancakes, popcorn, etc. Here's my recipe:

1/2 pound (2 sticks) unsalted butter, at room temperature

1 cup canola oil

1/4 teaspoon salt

With an electric mixer, mix the ingredients well. Put in a plastic tub, cover, and keep in the fridge. Another benefit is that it is always soft and spreadable.

Health Benefits

The fiber from the corn can help prevent constipation. The calcium in the cheese and milk help prevent osteoporosis, and the corn may help protect against macular degeneration and cancer, while strengthening the immune system. Onions are reported to protect against cancer and heart disease and the jalapeños speed up your metabolism to help burn calories. They also may thin the blood preventing clots.

Shopping List
fresh corn ▪ onion ▪ cheddar cheese ▪ jalapeño peppers ▪ cornmeal ▪ flour ▪ baking powder ▪ baking soda ▪ buttermilk ▪ canola oil ▪ eggs ▪ sugar

It's not always easy to photograph something light against something dark so this photo took me about three hours. I had four different lamps shining down on the corn bread, but at least it stayed warm so I could snack on it afterward.

"Blaster" Bran Muffins

There is no way you can compare these to any store-bought bran muffins. They are just sweet enough and are rich in flavor and fiber. Wheat bran is sometimes called "Miller's Bran" and I always find it at the health food store. Ground flaxseed meal is also available at most health food stores but make sure it's ground and not whole. You can also use chopped prunes instead of raisins to up the ante, or dried cranberries for some urinary tract support. I always grease muffin pans, even nonstick ones, which can sometimes play tug-of-war with the muffins.

1 1/2 cups all-purpose flour

1/2 cup sugar

2 teaspoons baking powder

1 teaspoon baking soda

1/2 teaspoon cinnamon

1/4 teaspoon salt

1 1/2 cups wheat bran

1/2 cup ground flaxseed meal

1 cup low-fat buttermilk

2 large eggs

1/3 cup canola oil

1/4 cup molasses

1 teaspoon vanilla extract

1/2 cup raisins (optional)

Start-to-Finish
30 minutes

Do I Have What It Takes?
You'll need a 12-cup muffin pan, preferably nonstick.

1 Preheat the oven to 400°F. Lightly grease a 12-cup muffin pan with butter.

2 Into a large bowl, sift together the flour, sugar, baking powder, baking soda, cinnamon, and salt. Add the bran and flaxseed meal and mix well.

3 In a small bowl or measuring cup, combine the buttermilk, eggs, oil, molasses, and vanilla. Add the buttermilk mixture to the flour mixture all at once and gently combine using a spatula or spoon. Fold in the raisins. Do not overmix.

4 Evenly divide the batter between 12 muffin cups and bake for 15 minutes, or 18 minutes for a crispier top. Immediately remove the muffins from the pan to a wire cooling rack.

Health Benefits

Fiber from wheat bran is a well-known antidote for constipation as well as weight loss, and may help reduce the risk of colon cancer. Flax provides omega-3s to protect your heart. Flax may also protect you against prostate and breast cancers, hypertension, arthritis, and macular degeneration, and don't be surprised if it helps make your hair shiny and your skin improves. Raisins and bran may also protect against hypertension, cancer, and heart disease.

Shopping List
flour ▪ sugar ▪ baking powder ▪ baking soda ▪ cinnamon ▪ wheat bran ▪ ground flaxseed meal ▪ buttermilk ▪ eggs ▪ canola oil ▪ molasses ▪ vanilla extract ▪ raisins

Everyone who comes over tries to lift the plate off this gorgeous mosaic table, but it's part of the design and is permanently glued down. The little knife came from a secondhand store and, before you chastise me for putting butter on my muffins, you should know that it's one of those new plant sterol spreads. As soon as I got this shot, I ate both the muffins with a glass of milk.

Soups for the Soul

Vegetable Micro-Miracle Soup

MAKES A HUGE POT OF SOUP

This may be the most important and valuable recipe in the book. By using a minimum of 15 different vegetables you get a huge variety of antioxidants and that's better than any vitamin pill. As with any soup, the better the stock, the better the soup, and this recipe can be made with either chicken, beef, or vegetable stock. It takes me about 25 minutes to prepare and chop all the vegetables. I listed the vegetables I used but you can choose whatever is in season. Try to get as many different colors as possible. I do not recommend beets or red cabbage because they will color your whole soup. By adding a can of drained beans, like lima or cannellini for protein, this soup becomes a meal in itself.

10 cups chicken, beef, or vegetable stock

1 diced handful each of:

- broccoli
- carrot
- asparagus
- potato
- turnip
- red bell pepper
- green beans
- wax beans
- zucchini
- celery
- snow peas
- onion

1 ear of corn, sliced off the cob

1 handful baby spinach

1 handful fresh-shelled peas

In a large soup pot over medium-high heat, bring the stock to a boil. Add all the vegetables and return to a boil. Reduce the heat to low, cover, and simmer for 15 minutes, making sure it stays gently bubbling. Test the hardest vegetable, usually the carrot, for doneness. Taste for salt and pepper, depending on your stock.

Kitchen Tip

Hold on to Your Wilted Old Vegetables

Toss them in the freezer along with leftover bones from roasted chicken or beef. When you accumulate enough you can make a delicious stock.

Health Benefits

This antiaging pot of goodness may provide protection against heart disease and memory loss as well as breast, lung, and prostate cancers. It can strengthen your bones and teeth, maintain your cholesterol, and boost your immune system. It may also help you avoid urinary tract infections and vision loss while helping maintain a healthy blood pressure.

Start-to-Finish
45 minutes

Do I Have What It Takes?
You'll need a large soup pot with a lid.

Shopping List
chicken, beef, or vegetable stock (preferably homemade)
- 15 different veggies

These great old soup bowls came from an antique shop in Pasadena and they are on a beaded place mat that I use at Christmastime. The hardest part of this photo was keeping that piece of asparagus afloat.

Roasted Tomato Soup MAKES 6 TO 8 SERVINGS

Everyone will be talking about your tomato soup! So tomato-ey, so delicious, and super nutritious. To kick it into overdrive, use a good homemade chicken stock. You can save time by preheating the stock in advance. As for the canned tomatoes, I like the boxes of Pomi brand strained tomatoes if you can find them, but most canned varieties will do. Cooked tomatoes are an excellent source of lycopene, but don't skip the olive oil because they need a little fat for it to absorb well. If you love your man and want to help keep his prostate healthy, serve him this soup. I love to eat this over cooked rice and then add about a teaspoon of real cream.

4 to 5 large tomatoes, cut into quarters

1 tablespoon plus 1 teaspoon olive oil

Salt and pepper to taste

1 cup chopped onion

2 cloves garlic, minced

3 cups chicken or vegetable stock or water, heated

One 26-ounce box Pomi strained tomatoes, or one 28-ounce can diced tomatoes in juice

1 bay leaf

$^1/_2$ teaspoon salt

Black pepper to taste

7 or 8 whole large basil leaves (about $^1/_3$ cup)

1 Preheat the oven to 400°F.

2 Place the fresh tomatoes on a large baking sheet and toss with 1 tablespoon of the olive oil and a little salt and pepper. Roast for 45 minutes, stirring once.

3 While the tomatoes are roasting, in a large soup pot, heat the remaining 1 teaspoon of olive oil over medium heat. Add the onion and garlic and cook, stirring occasionally, until the onion is softened and translucent, about 5 minutes.

4 Add the hot stock or water, boxed (or canned) tomatoes, bay leaf, $^1/_2$ teaspoon salt, and pepper. Bring to a boil, then reduce the heat, cover, and simmer for 30 minutes.

5 Stir the roasted tomatoes into the pot and simmer for another 5 or 10 minutes. You may have to raise the temperature a bit to get it bubbling again.

6 Remove the pot from the heat and add the fresh basil leaves. Let the soup cool for 5 minutes and puree slightly in a food processor, blender, or with an immersion (stick) blender. Garnish with a few strips of basil.

Health Benefits

The big story about tomatoes, particularly cooked ones, is cancer protection, especially prostate cancer. Tomatoes may also protect you from macular degeneration, heart disease, and memory loss and could give you a stronger immune system and urinary tract. They have even been reported to alleviate menopause symptoms and prevent wrinkles caused by the sun.

Shopping List
fresh tomatoes ▪ olive oil ▪ onion ▪ garlic ▪ chicken or vegetable stock (optional) ▪ boxed or canned tomatoes ▪ bay leaf ▪ fresh basil

I found this fabulous soup bowl at the mall in a Williams-Sonoma store and the basil on top of the soup came from my own garden. The spoon is from a store that sold antiques and collectibles and the fabric was leftover from a sewing project.

Beans 'n' Greens Soup

MAKES 4 SERVINGS

Choose from several health-giving greens like collards, chard, kale, bok choy, spinach, or mustard greens, or combine whatever you have on hand. For the photo I used collards, kale, and chard. A taller, deeper soup pot is best for making this soup, to accommodate the flavor bundle. It's hard to be exact about the cooking time, so start checking the beans for tenderness after about 45 minutes and adjust your time accordingly. You can soak the beans overnight to save some cooking time. Just cover the beans with cold water, let stand overnight, then discard the soaking water, drain, and rinse the beans. By soaking you'll cut about 15 minutes of cooking time and the beans will produce a bit less gas. So, soak if you want to. You can either cut the cooking time or cut the cheese... your call.

FLAVOR BUNDLE

1 medium carrot

$1/2$ celery stalk

$1/4$ medium onion

1 clove garlic, halved

2 sprigs fresh parsley

1 sprig fresh thyme

1 bay leaf

5 black peppercorns

SOUP

1 cup dried white beans, like Great Northern

6 cups water

1 tablespoon olive oil

2 cups finely chopped greens (see Headnote)

$1/2$ teaspoon salt

Black pepper to taste

1 Spread open a piece of cheesecloth about 2 feet square. Place the carrot, celery, onion, garlic, parsley, thyme, bay leaf, and peppercorns in the center and bundle it all up. Tie it securely with kitchen string.

2 Examine the beans thoroughly, discarding any stones and broken beans. Wash and rinse well.

3 Place the beans, water, oil, and flavor bundle in a large soup pot. Bring to a boil, reduce the heat, cover, and simmer over low heat for about 1 hour, or until beans are almost done (45 minutes if you soak the beans overnight).

Here's what your flavor bundle should look like—not too fat so it stays under water and tied up nice and secure.

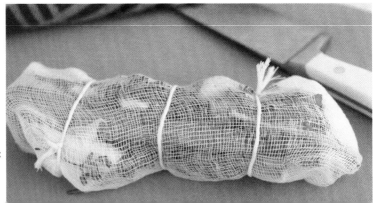

4 Remove the flavor bundle. Add the greens and cook for another 15 minutes. Remove 1 bean and taste for doneness. If it's not soft enough, cook another 5 to 10 minutes. Season with salt and pepper to taste.

Health Benefits

The soluble fiber in beans can lower your cholesterol and stabilize blood sugar so it's recommended for diabetics. Beans may also help prevent high blood pressure, heart disease, cancer, and stroke. The greens may protect you from cancer, heart disease, and osteoporosis as well as cataracts and macular degeneration.

Start-to-Finish
1 hour and 30 minutes, mostly unattended

Do I Have What It Takes?
You'll need a large soup pot, cheesecloth, and kitchen string.

Shopping List
carrot ▪ celery ▪ onion ▪ garlic ▪ fresh parsley ▪ fresh thyme ▪ bay leaf ▪ black peppercorns ▪ dried white beans ▪ olive oil ▪ greens

I'm always on the lookout for interesting plates and bowls and this one had a distressed look that I liked. For a more dramatic picture I put more beans and less broth into the bowl than usual because the beans kept sinking to the bottom.

Corn Chowder Makes 4 to 6 servings

This delicious soup doesn't require much effort except for cutting off the fresh corn kernels. Just use a sharp knife and do it in a tall bowl to avoid creating corn wallpaper. Then use the dull side of the knife to scrape down all the juicy stuff you missed with the blade. Keep in mind that as tasty as white corn is, yellow corn has more health-building carotenoids. Use red, green, or yellow bell peppers or a colorful combination of all three. If you use frozen corn, it's already cooked so just add it with the milk, but it won't taste like fresh. If you're lucky enough to find freshly picked sweet summer corn at a local farm stand, you'll swear you could eat this soup for dessert.

1 tablespoon olive oil

1 cup diced onion

1/2 cup diced celery

1/4 teaspoon dried thyme leaves

1 cup diced red bell pepper

1 1/2 cups water or chicken stock

2 cups fresh yellow corn kernels (3 or 4 ears)

1 cup diced potatoes, about 1/4 inch thick

1 bay leaf

1/2 cup 1% low-fat milk

2 teaspoons all-purpose flour

1/4 teaspoon salt

Black pepper to taste

Start-to-Finish
45 minutes

Do I Have What It Takes?
No special equipment is needed.

1   In a medium soup pot, heat the oil over medium heat. Add the onion, celery, and thyme and cook, stirring, for 2 minutes. Add the bell pepper and cook another 2 minutes, stirring once or twice.

2   Add the water or stock, corn, potatoes, and bay leaf. Bring to a boil, cover, reduce the heat, and simmer for 10 minutes.

3   In a small bowl or measuring cup, whisk together the milk and flour until smooth and add to the pot with the salt and pepper. Combine well, cover, and cook for another 5 minutes.

⌒ Kitchen Tip

Skimming Fat off the Top of Chilled Soup

After skimming off the fat with a large spoon, lay a paper towel on the soup, press on it a little, and it will absorb all the last bits of fat.

Health Benefits

Yellow corn and onions may reduce the risk of cancer, high blood pressure, and stroke. Corn can boost your estrogen level and protect your eye health as well. Red bell peppers are reported to defend against cancer, arthritis, asthma, and coronary artery disease. Onions are good for your heart, cholesterol, circulation, and memory and may help to ward off infections. They may also protect against cancer and help the liver eliminate toxins.

Shopping List
olive oil ▪ onion ▪ celery ▪ dried thyme leaves ▪ red bell pepper ▪ chicken stock (optional) ▪ fresh corn ▪ potato ▪ bay leaf ▪ milk ▪ flour

The white crackled table is actually a tray that sits in my bedroom. The plate came from a secondhand store and behind is one of my kitchen towels. To hold the spoon up I stacked two cans and wedged the spoon handle in between.

Black Bean Soup MAKES 2 SERVINGS

This thick and yummy soup goes beautifully with my Jalapeño Corn Bread (see page 48). It's all you need for a perfect lunch that will keep your blood sugar steady all afternoon. To me the best texture is achieved when you puree about half of the soup and pour it back into the pot. As with all beans, examine them carefully before cooking and look for errant stones or pebbles. I spread them out on paper towels and throw away any broken or damaged beans. New research indicates that of all the beans out there, black beans are the highest in antioxidants. I love to cook soups and usually make them in the evening and refrigerate them for the next day.

1 cup dried black beans

2 teaspoons olive oil

$^1/_2$ cup chopped celery

$^1/_2$ cup chopped onion

$^1/_2$ cup diced green bell pepper

1 clove garlic, minced

$^1/_2$ teaspoon chili powder

$^1/_2$ teaspoon dried oregano

$^1/_4$ teaspoon cumin

3 cups water

1 bay leaf

$^1/_2$ teaspoon salt

Black pepper to taste

Juice of $^1/_2$ lime (about 2 teaspoons)

Fresh cilantro (optional), for garnish

1 Examine the beans carefully, discarding any pebbles or bad and broken ones. Rinse the beans and set aside.

2 In a medium soup pot, heat the oil over medium heat. Add the celery, onion, bell pepper, garlic, chili powder, oregano, and cumin. Cook, stirring occasionally, until the vegetables soften, about 5 minutes.

3 Add the water, beans, and bay leaf. Bring to a boil, then reduce the heat, cover, and simmer for about 1 hour and 15 minutes.

4 Remove the bay leaf and add the salt, pepper, and lime juice. For a thicker soup, puree half of it in a food processor, blender, or with an immersion (stick) blender. Serve plain or with some fresh cilantro on top.

Health Benefits

Eating black beans can definitely lower your cholesterol, which can help you avoid heart disease. They may also lower your blood pressure and protect you against cancer. Since beans help keep blood sugar on an even keel, they are also recommended for diabetics. The onions can improve circulation and memory and green peppers may help prevent macular degeneration, heart disease, and cancer. Peppers are also recommended for asthmatics.

Start-to-Finish
1 hour and 30 minutes, mostly unattended

Do I Have What It Takes?
You'll need a medium soup pot with a lid and a food processor, blender, or immersion blender.

Shopping List
dried black beans ▪ olive oil ▪ celery ▪ onion ▪ green bell pepper ▪ garlic ▪ chili powder ▪ oregano ▪ cumin ▪ bay leaf ▪ lime ▪ fresh cilantro (optional)

It's true that black bean soup won't be winning any beauty contests but I

wanted to show how thick and yummy it is. The bowl is resting on the underside of a

quilted place mat I found at Anthropologie.

Cream of Broccoli Soup

MAKES 4 SERVINGS

There's no cream in this rich and healthful soup. The secret thickening ingredient is rice, although you can stir in a tablespoon of cream just before serving. A good home-made chicken stock will give you the best-tasting soup and heating your stock in advance speeds up the cooking time. It's important to find ways to include broccoli in your diet. This soup can be an appetizer *and* one of your five-a-day vegetables.

1 teaspoon olive oil

$^1/_2$ cup chopped onion

2 tablespoons long-grain rice

1$^1/_2$ cups chicken or vegetable stock, heated

$^1/_4$ teaspoon salt

Black pepper to taste

2 cups fresh broccoli florets

Start-to-Finish
40 minutes

Do I Have What It Takes?
You'll need a soup pot with a lid and a food processor, blender, or immersion (stick) blender.

Shopping List
olive oil ▪ onion ▪ long-grain rice ▪ chicken or vegetable stock ▪ broccoli

1. In a soup pot, heat the oil over medium heat. Add the onion and cook, stirring occasionally, until softened, about 3 minutes.

2. Add the rice, hot stock, salt, and pepper and bring to a boil. Reduce the heat to low, cover, and simmer for 20 minutes.

3. Stir in the broccoli and return to a boil. Cover and cook for another 5 minutes.

4. Let the soup cool slightly, then puree in a food processor or blender or with an immersion (stick) blender. Add a little extra stock or water if the soup is too thick for your taste.

Health Benefits

Research strongly suggests that broccoli can help reduce the risk of cancer. It can also protect your eyes and heart and boost your immune system. It even provides calcium to help fight osteoporosis.

It's really a big coffee cup I found at Bloomingdale's, but today it's a soup mug.

The spoon came from an antique mall and the wicker tray from a shop on Ventura

Boulevard, in Los Angeles. Oops, you can see a reflection of my lights in the mug!

Beet and Cabbage Borscht

MAKES 6 TO 8 SERVINGS

It looks like my Polish roots are showing. Poles traditionally stir a little sour cream into their borscht. My dad used to eat his borscht with a side of mashed potatoes. With his soup spoon he took a little scoop of potatoes, then dipped it in the soup so every bite had a combination of both. As with most soups all of the vegetable measurements are approximate, so a little more or less of any of the chopped vegetables will be fine. The cabbage can be shredded with a food processor, box grater, or knife. The vegetables should be diced no more than $1/2$ inch thick. There's a lot of chopping but otherwise, it's easy as pie. Actually pie is not easy at all, so let's just say it's easy. When you purchase fresh beets, they come with the greens attached so use them (except for any tough big leaves) for the greens. A good homemade beef or chicken stock really adds to this complex and delicious soup.

1 tablespoon olive oil

1 cup chopped onion

1 cup chopped celery

6 cups beef, chicken, or vegetable stock, or water

$1^1/2$ cups diced fresh beets

1 cup chopped beet greens

2 cups shredded cabbage

1 cup diced carrot

1 cup diced red or new potato

1 cup canned tomato puree

$1/4$ cup chopped fresh dill

1 tablespoon cider vinegar

1 tablespoon sugar

1 teaspoon caraway seeds

$1^1/2$ teaspoons salt

Black pepper to taste

1. In a large soup pot, heat the olive oil over medium heat. Add the onion and celery and cook, stirring a few times, until the onion is translucent, about 3 minutes.

2. Add the remaining ingredients, bring to a boil, then reduce heat, cover, and cook at a gentle low boil for about 25 minutes.

Health Benefits

Beets are an antiaging powerhouse. They are said to stabilize blood sugar and cholesterol, support the liver, and help fight heart disease and cancer. Beet greens may even help you quit smoking. The rich variety of other vegetables can protect against prostate, lung, and other cancers; heart disease; macular degeneration; and memory loss. They can also boost your immune system and protect the urinary tract.

Start-to-Finish
I hour

Do I Have What It Takes?
Yes, if you have a big soup pot with a lid.

Shopping List
olive oil ▪ onion ▪ celery ▪ beef, chicken, or vegetable stock ▪ beets with their greens ▪ cabbage ▪ carrot ▪ potato ▪ canned tomato puree ▪ fresh dill ▪ cider vinegar ▪ sugar ▪ caraway seeds

To show the soup spoon (try saying that 5 times!) I kept trying to rest the handle of the spoon on the edge of the bowl. It sank every time. So I rigged it by burying a little candle holder in the soup to hold it up. The colorful cloth was a souvenir I brought home from a trip to my family's homeland, Poland.

Chicken Soup

You can do so much with a big pot of chicken soup. Have it with noodles or rice, or use it as stock for other soups, like vegetable or bean. Give some to a friend with a cold (I'm convinced it works), or freeze it in ice cube trays—store the cubes in freezer bags and use them as needed. There's always a bag of chicken cubes in my freezer, which I use to make chili, rice pilaf, gravies, or other soups. Don't even talk to me about store-bought bouillon cubes—just look at the list of ingredients! My philosophy is if I can't pronounce it... I don't eat it. If you don't feel like chopping vegetables you can leave them whole. I always used to see a big whole carrot in my Polish mother's soup pot. It's best to make this the day before serving. That way you can remove all the fat, which will rise to the top once it's chilled.

3 pounds chicken parts: wings, backs, necks, or some of each

3 quarts cold water

1/2 onion, cut in quarters

I large carrot, cut in large chunks

I stalk celery, cut in large chunks

I small parsnip, cut in large chunks

Handful of fresh parsley

I sprig fresh thyme (or 1/2 teaspoon dried)

I clove garlic, cut in half

I bay leaf

1 1/2 teaspoons salt

4 or 5 whole black peppercorns

1   In a large pot, put washed chicken parts with just enough water to cover. Bring to a boil, let it boil for 1 minute, then discard the water and rinse the chicken with cold water. This process usually eliminates the need to skim any unsightly foam off the top.

2   Add the 3 quarts of cold water to the rinsed chicken in the pot, then add the remaining ingredients. Bring to a boil, reduce the heat, cover, and simmer for 2 hours.

3   Using a large colander over a large bowl (you may need 2 bowls), strain the soup, discarding all the solids including the chicken parts and vegetables. Cover and let the bowl(s) of soup cool for about an hour, then refrigerate overnight.

4   In the morning remove the fat, which will have settled on the surface, with a large spoon. To finish removing every last bit of fat try pressing a paper towel on the surface—it will lift the remaining fat right off.

Health Benefits

They don't call it "Jewish Penicillin" for nothing. I'm convinced that chicken soup helps to ease cold and flu symptoms. Even when you're not under the weather, the nutrients from the vegetables, which wind up in the broth, can boost your immune system and help protect you from cancer and heart disease.

Start-to-Finish
2 hours and 30 minutes, mostly unattended

Do I Have What It Takes?
You'll need a large soup pot and large colander.

Shopping List
chicken parts ▪ onion ▪ carrot ▪ celery ▪ parsnip, fresh parsley ▪ thyme ▪ garlic ▪ bay leaf ▪ whole peppercorns

Salads for Sure

Antioxidant Slaw   MAKES 4 SERVINGS

Think of this salad as your nutritional insurance policy. By eating lots of different colors of produce you get the widest range of health benefits. The vegetables can be prepared any way you like—chopped, diced, shredded, chunky, or let a food processor do all the work. I prefer them shredded so nobody tries to i.d. any one item: "What's this? Spinach? I hate spinach!" Not a problem if it's disguised as dark green lettuce.

1/2 cup each shredded:

romaine lettuce

fresh spinach

red bell pepper

yellow bell pepper

red cabbage

carrot

1/4 cup chopped red onion

DRESSING

1 tablespoon extra virgin olive oil

1 tablespoon balsamic vinegar

1/4 teaspoon Dijon mustard

Pinch of salt and black pepper

Start-to-Finish
about 15 minutes

Do I Have What It Takes?
No special equipment is needed.

Shopping List
romaine lettuce ▪ spinach ▪ red bell pepper ▪ yellow bell pepper ▪ red cabbage ▪ carrot ▪ red onion ▪ olive oil ▪ balsamic vinegar ▪ Dijon mustard

1 In a large salad bowl, add all of the vegetables, including the onion.

2 To make the dressing, in a small bowl, whisk together the oil, vinegar, mustard, salt, and pepper. Add the dressing to the vegetables and toss thoroughly for about a minute.

Health Benefits

Where do I start? This kaleidoscope of color can protect against vision loss, macular degeneration, high cholesterol, high blood pressure, blood clots, and memory loss. It may also strengthen the immune system and urinary tract, improve circulation, and help fight infection, heart disease, and breast, prostate, and lung cancers, as well as strengthen teeth and bones.

Kitchen Tip

Cut the Tops Off Carrots Right Away

If the tops are left on they will continue to draw moisture and nutrients out of the carrots.

Proof again that discount stores make for some great finds. This unique plate cost next to nothing but looked so rich, especially when I put it on a silk tablecloth that I already had. The challenge with this picture was getting the reflection on the edges of that glass plate.

Splendiferous Cruciferous Salad

MAKES 4 TO 6 SERVINGS

By now most of us have heard that cruciferous vegetables are believed to reduce the risk of cancer. They include cabbage, Brussels sprouts, broccoli, radishes, cauliflower, turnips, and certain greens. There's a triple dose in this vibrant, colorful salad.

I cup shredded green cabbage

I cup shredded red cabbage

I cup sliced or shredded radishes

$1/2$ cup thinly sliced yellow bell pepper

DRESSING

I tablespoon extra virgin olive oil

I tablespoon cider vinegar

$1/2$ teaspoon sugar

$1/8$ teaspoon celery seeds

$1/8$ teaspoon salt

Black pepper to taste

Start-to-Finish
15 minutes

Do I Have What It Takes?
A box grater makes shredding easy, as does a food processor, but a sharp knife will also do the job.

Shopping List
green cabbage ▪ red cabbage ▪ radishes ▪ yellow bell pepper ▪ olive oil ▪ cider vinegar ▪ sugar ▪ celery seeds

1. In a large bowl, add all of the vegetables.

2. To make the dressing, in a small bowl, whisk together the oil, vinegar, sugar, celery seeds, salt, and pepper. Add the dressing to the vegetables and toss well.

Health Benefits

There is very strong evidence that cruciferous vegetables can help reduce the risk of cancer. The added yellow bell pepper may protect your eyes, lungs, and heart.

I admit that I stood the radishes up for the picture, and I didn't see the

little piece of red cabbage on the table until later. The table, by the way, sits

near my front door entry. To get the pretty reflections behind the bowl I set two crystal

glasses way in the back and shone a separate light on them.

Bean Salad   MAKES 6 TO 8 SERVINGS

One important thing about bean salad is to make it in advance so it has a chance to marinate. Overnight is best, but refrigerate it for at least an hour before serving. My bean salad is never the same twice and yours can change, too. Other ideas include fresh cooked yellow wax beans; canned black or lima beans; orange, yellow, or green bell peppers; celery; olives; grape tomatoes; green onions (scallions); garlic. There are dozens of different combinations. Another thing I like to do is add a scoop of bean salad to my dinner salad for protein and extra fiber.

$1/4$ pound fresh green beans

$1/2$ red bell pepper, chopped

$1/2$ cup chopped red onion

One 15-ounce can red kidney beans, drained and rinsed

One 15-ounce can cannellini beans, drained and rinsed

One 8-ounce can garbanzo beans, drained and rinsed

1 tablespoon chopped fresh parsley

DRESSING

$1/4$ cup canola oil

2 tablespoons red wine vinegar

$1/2$ teaspoon Dijon mustard

1 clove garlic, minced

$1/4$ teaspoon salt

Black pepper to taste

Start-to-Finish
20 minutes, plus 1 hour refrigeration

1   Cut the green beans into 1-inch pieces and steam or boil until crisp-tender, about 5 minutes. Drain well.

2   In a large bowl, combine the cooked green beans, red bell pepper, onion, kidney beans, cannellini beans, garbanzo beans, and parsley.

3   To make the dressing, in a small bowl, whisk together the oil, vinegar, mustard, garlic, salt, and pepper. Add the dressing to the vegetables and beans and toss well. Cover and refrigerate from 1 hour to overnight. Serve with a slotted spoon.

Health Benefits

Beans provide important fiber that can lower your cholesterol and blood pressure, and protect you from heart disease, hypertension, cancer, diabetes, constipation, and hemorrhoids. They also provide calcium for strong bones and teeth. The red bell pepper helps to burn fat and can also protect you from heart disease, cancer, cataracts, and macular degeneration as well as arthritis, and asthma. Then there's the red onion, which is reported to prevent blood clots and heart disease, lower cholesterol and blood pressure, improve circulation and memory, and support the liver.

Do I Have What It Takes?
No special equipment is needed.

Shopping List
fresh green beans ▪ red bell pepper ▪ red onion ▪ canned red kidney beans ▪ canned cannellini beans ▪ canned garbanzo beans, fresh parsley ▪ canola oil, red wine vinegar ▪ Dijon mustard ▪ garlic

I chose one of my favorite plates for this bean salad. Then I placed it on a larger green tin plate that came from an antique shop. This salad is a beautiful combination of colors and textures, and the enticing smell of the onions and dressing was making me hungry. I may have lifted a few beans off the plate.

Beet Salad

MAKES 4 TO 6 SERVINGS

First thing . . . remove any white clothing you may be wearing. Second . . . put on some latex gloves. Third . . . put down some waxed paper or paper towels to work on. You might as well work with red paint but it's the vegetables with intense colors that have all the phytochemicals. I know they're messy but fresh beets are a zillion times better tasting than canned ones and steaming them preserves more vitamins than boiling. If you can only find small beets, just use more of them as long as you wind up with about 4 cups when diced. And if you're lucky as I was you might find beautiful golden beets to mix and match. Remember to save the nutritious greens for other cooking.

3 beets (tennis ball size)

DRESSING

1 tablespoon extra virgin
  olive oil

1 tablespoon balsamic vinegar

2 tablespoons fresh orange
  juice

$1/2$ teaspoon sugar

$1/8$ teaspoon salt

Black pepper to taste

Start-to-Finish
1 hour

Do I Have What It Takes?
A vegetable steamer is
helpful but not necessary.

Shopping List
fresh beets ▪ olive oil ▪
balsamic vinegar ▪ orange ▪
sugar

1 Cut the leaves off the beets, leaving 1 inch of the stems attached. Do not peel, but scrub the beets well under cold water. Steam or boil the whole beets until done, 30 to 45 minutes, depending on the size. Baby-size beets may only take 15 minutes, so keep checking them. Test by piercing with a thin knife (a fork lets out too much juice).

2 Meanwhile, to prepare the dressing, in a small bowl, combine the oil, vinegar, orange juice, sugar, salt, and pepper. Set aside.

3 Remove the peel from the cooked beets, which will slip off easily, and trim both ends. Chop the warm beets into bite-size pieces and transfer to a glass bowl. (Plastic will retain the red dye.)

4 Pour dressing over warm beets, toss, and refrigerate until ready to serve.

Health Benefits

Beets have strong antiaging properties. They can protect your immune system, liver, memory, eyes, heart, and urinary tract. As with other red vegetables, beets can also protect against prostate and other cancers, and might help alleviate menopause symptoms.

Yes, these are all beets. At the health food store I was lucky to find some beautiful golden beets along with the red ones for this picture. By turning the plate to the exact right spot, I got the nice reflections that you see. What you can't see is the design of the plate, which is a spider web, though it does reflect a little bit on the pink fabric.

Tomato and Onion Salad

MAKES 4 SERVINGS, BUT I HAVE EATEN THE ENTIRE BOWL

There's something about combining the sweetness of tomatoes with the edginess of green onions that sends me into hog heaven. Remember when they just had red and round tomatoes at the market? Well now you can find orange and yellow ones, heirloom, striped, Italian plum, on the vine, in a bag, red grape, yellow grape, cherry, and even high-lycopene hybrids. This means you can create a beautiful multicolored salad that's full of health-promoting phytonutrients. It's best to chop the tomatoes first so they have a chance to drain and then prepare the onions and dressing. If you don't like onion, or if it doesn't like you, try substituting some fresh basil. Here's the key for a knockout tomato salad: Don't refrigerate the tomatoes, ever. It diminishes their texture and flavor. So try to make this salad last minute—it's really worth it.

4 cups coarsely chopped tomatoes, or small ones left whole

$^1/_2$ cup chopped green onions (scallions), including the white part

DRESSING

1 tablespoon balsamic vinegar

1 teaspoon extra virgin olive oil

Pinch of salt

Black pepper to taste

Start-to-Finish
10 minutes

Do I Have What It Takes?
A colander is helpful.

1 Place the chopped tomatoes into a colander and let the juices drain out while you prepare the other ingredients. You can also drain them on paper towels.

2 In a large bowl, add the drained tomatoes and onions.

3 To make the dressing, in a small bowl, whisk together the vinegar, oil, salt, and pepper. Add to the tomatoes and toss well. Serve immediately. Do not refrigerate.

Health Benefits

Red tomatoes are often recommended in the fight against cancer. All tomatoes and onions are reported to protect your heart, memory, and immune system. Tomatoes may also strengthen the urinary tract and prevent macular degeneration. Onions may thin the blood, prevent clots, lower cholesterol and blood pressure, improve circulation, and help fight infections.

Shopping List
tomatoes ▪ green onions ▪ balsamic vinegar ▪ olive oil

For the first time in my life I grew some tomatoes in the backyard and decided it was the perfect backdrop for my tomato salad. I actually grew the tiny yellow pear tomatoes and the quartered red ones in the salad. Here, I was holding the plate in one hand and snapping my picture with the other.

*H*ere are a few dressing recipes that can be served with any combination of your favorite salad ingredients. I mix most of my salad dressings right in a jar, and right before pouring, I shake the jar like a bartender making a martini.

Balsamic Dressing   MAKES ¹/₄ CUP

The time it takes you to read this paragraph is the amount of time it takes to make this dressing. I swear, in the time it takes to open a bottle of store-bought salad glue— I mean bottled dressing—you could be enjoying the kind of quality dressing you get in fine restaurants. This dressing is so good you don't even need salt or pepper. The only thing easier than this is if I come over and make it for you.

2 tablespoons olive oil

2 tablespoons balsamic vinegar

In a small bowl or in a jar, combine the oil and vinegar.

Honey Mustard Dressing

MAKES ABOUT 1 CUP

I think you'll find just the right amount of sweetness in this super creamy and easy-to-make dressing. Cream-style honey is available in most supermarkets. It's white in color and has the consistency of peanut butter, but you can also use regular honey.

In a small glass or metal bowl using an electric hand mixer on low speed, combine the vinegar, mustard, and honey. While mixing, add the oil in a slow steady stream. Add the salt and pepper.

$1/3$ cup white wine vinegar

2 tablespoons Dijon mustard

$1/4$ cup cream-style honey

$1/4$ cup extra virgin olive oil

$1/8$ teaspoon salt

Black pepper to taste

Italian Dressing

MAKES ABOUT $1/3$ CUP

You can find "Italian" Seasoning in the supermarket. I use it all the time because it usually has the perfect combination of marjoram, thyme, rosemary, sage, oregano, and basil. I keep leftover dressing refrigerated in a jar, but since olive oil solidifies when chilled, I take it out an hour in advance to warm it up to room temperature. If I forget, then I microwave it for about 5 seconds.

In a small bowl, whisk together the oil, vinegar, sugar, seasoning, salt, and pepper. Stir just before pouring.

2 tablespoons extra virgin olive oil

$1/4$ cup red wine vinegar

$3/4$ teaspoon sugar

$1/4$ teaspoon Italian Seasoning

$1/8$ teaspoon salt

Black pepper to taste

Pomegranate Dressing

MAKES ABOUT ¹/₄ CUP

If you can get your hands on some pomegranate molasses or syrup, you're in for a treat. Most Middle Eastern groceries sell them, and you can also find them online. Pomegranates, which are in season in the fall, are just full of antioxidants. This way you can get some of their health benefits all year long as well as some of that unique sweet and tart taste of pomegranates.

2 tablespoons pomegranate molasses or syrup

2 tablespoons red wine vinegar

1 tablespoon olive oil

¹/₈ teaspoon salt

Black pepper to taste

In a small bowl, whisk together the molasses, vinegar, oil, salt, and pepper. Stir just before pouring.

Dips and Snacks

Caramelized Onion and Roasted Red Pepper Dip

MAKES 2 1/2 CUPS

I absolutely love this dip. It was a favorite of my "pit crew," the terrific people who did my makeup, hair, and wardrobe at the *Jenny Jones Show* in Chicago. I invited them over every year to watch the Academy Awards and always served this dip. Imagine the fun of watching the awards with people who specialize in makeup, hair, and wardrobe. The most fun was the year that my hairdresser, Ricardo, showed up in drag at my front door. Let me tell you, this was not a pretty woman. I miss you, Ricardo! Now back to my dip.

Everyone asks me for this recipe, but I warn them that it's easy to make but it does take time. . . 3 hours to cook the onions down, but you can always do laundry or your taxes, or watch a couple of movies. You'll need a pan with tall sides and a lid because the sliced onions measure a whopping 6 to 8 cups, though they cook down to about a cup. The longer you cook them the smaller they get, but they also turn sweeter and darker. It's best to make this the day before so the flavors blend overnight. Bottled roasted red peppers are fine for this recipe, and the big sweet onions like Vidalia or Maui are ideal. In the photo, I used red onions, which added to the pretty pink color.

I serve this dip with sliced vegetables and reduced-fat potato chips. Crispy bagel chips or breadsticks would also be good.

1 teaspoon olive oil

2 large sweet onions, sliced
 1/2 inch thick

2 tablespoons red wine
 vinegar

1 teaspoon sugar

1 teaspoon salt

Black pepper to taste

1 cup reduced-fat sour cream
 (8 ounces)

1 In a large sauté pan, heat the oil over medium heat. Add the onions and cook, stirring a few times as they reduce in volume, for about 10 minutes.

2 Add the vinegar, sugar, salt, and pepper. Cover, reduce the heat to low and cook for 3 hours, stirring every 30 minutes. The onions are done when the liquid has evaporated, the mixture is dark and sticky, and it measures about a cup. If you still have liquid in the pan after 3 hours, just raise the temperature and cook uncovered until the liquid evaporates.

3 Remove from the heat and transfer to a dinner plate to cool. Place the cooled onions in a food processor fitted with the metal blade. Add the sour cream, yogurt, and red pepper after patting it dry. Process until smooth. Cover and refrigerate before serving.

Health Benefits

The onions and peppers in this dip can protect you against heart disease, improve your memory, thin your blood, and also provide cancer protection. They also support eye health, and peppers are good for those with arthritis and asthma.

$1/2$ cup fat-free plain yogurt

$1/2$ of a jarred roasted red pepper, patted dry

Start-to-Finish
3 hours and 15 minutes, mostly unattended

Do I Have What It Takes?
You'll need a large sauté pan with a lid, a food processor, and a free evening.

Shopping List
olive oil ▪ sweet onions ▪ red wine vinegar ▪ sugar ▪ reduced-fat sour cream ▪ fat-free plain yogurt ▪ jarred roasted red peppers

I borrowed from everywhere for this picture. The glass container for the dip is part of a "chip and dip" set I had in the kitchen and the saucer is actually a candle holder that was in the bathroom. The crystal glasses were a gift that I keep in the dining room hutch, and the tablecloth was just a piece of fabric I found on sale.

Tomato Salsa **MAKES 2 TO 4 SERVINGS**

There's nothing like freshly made tomato salsa, also known as *pico de gallo*. No matter how much I make, it always disappears. It's easy to double or triple the ingredient quantities so you can make a bigger batch. The best flavor will come from ripe, firm tomatoes that have not been refrigerated, so it's best to make this right before serving. Dice the tomatoes first, remove the seeds, and place them in a colander to drain, while preparing the rest of the ingredients.

I cup fresh diced tomatoes, seeded and drained

$1/3$ cup diced onion

$1/4$ cup diced jalapeño pepper

I tablespoon fresh cilantro

I teaspoon fresh lemon juice (lime juice works, too)

$1/4$ teaspoon salt

Black pepper to taste

Start-to-Finish
10 minutes

Do I Have What It Takes?
No special equipment is needed.

Shopping List
tomato ▪ onion ▪ jalapeño pepper ▪ fresh cilantro ▪ lemon

In a medium bowl, combine the ingredients and watch it disappear.

Health Benefits

Tomatoes may help prevent prostate cancer, heart disease, and macular degeneration. They may also help maintain a healthy urinary tract, better memory, and stronger immune system. Onions may prevent blood clots, lower cholesterol and blood pressure, and help your body fight infections. They support your heart and liver, strengthen capillaries, and may prevent memory loss, heart disease, and cancer. Chile peppers are good for arthritis, asthma, and better eye health and blood pressure. They also speed up your metabolism to help with weight loss.

I'm not sure exactly what the design is on this vibrant fabric, but it looked

Mexican to me, so I bought half a yard. It was just the look I wanted to go with my

discount store clay bowl and my fresh and fabulous salsa.

Black Bean Dip

Sometimes you've just got to have some dip, so why not have one that does you some good... as long as you dip with baked or reduced-fat chips, or veggies. A food processor is the perfect tool for this job but you can also use a blender or even a potato masher. If you have some latex gloves, wear them when you chop the jalapeños. If you don't and touch your eyes... you'll be sorrrrrry. To turn this into a Monster Bean Dip, just throw in a little hot sauce, or a lot, depending on what you have to prove.

1 teaspoon olive oil

$3/4$ cup diced onion

$1/2$ cup diced red bell pepper

2 jalapeño peppers, seeded and diced (about $1/2$ cup)

1 large clove garlic, minced

$1/4$ teaspoon cumin

One 15-ounce can black beans, drained, but not rinsed

2 ounces shredded reduced-fat Monterey Jack cheese ($1/2$ cup)

1 tablespoon fresh cilantro

1 teaspoon fresh lime juice

1 teaspoon balsamic vinegar

$1/4$ teaspoon salt

Black pepper to taste

1   In a medium sauté pan, heat the olive oil over medium heat. Add the onion, bell pepper, jalapeños, garlic, and cumin and cook, stirring, for 3 minutes. Add the black beans and cheese, stirring, until the cheese is melted, about 1 minute.

2   Remove from the heat and cool slightly. Place the bean mixture into a food processor fitted with a metal blade. Add the cilantro, lime juice, balsamic vinegar, salt, and pepper. Pulse about 5 times for a chunkier dip (my preference) or puree for 10 seconds for a smoother texture.

Health Benefits

The beans provide calcium to help prevent osteoporosis and soluble fiber for helping to stabilize blood sugar, especially good for diabetics. Beans are known to reduce cholesterol levels and may also protect against hypertension, high blood pressure, cancer, and heart disease. Onions, garlic, and bell peppers may help prevent blood clots, certain cancers, memory loss, and heart disease. They may also improve circulation, lower your blood pressure and cholesterol, and protect against arthritis, asthma, cataracts, and macular degeneration. Chile peppers can increase your metabolism to burn more calories.

Start-to-Finish
25 minutes

Do I Have What It Takes?
A food processor is helpful and latex gloves are good for handling hot chile peppers.

Shopping List
olive oil ■ onion ■ red bell pepper ■ jalapeño peppers ■ fresh garlic ■ cumin ■ canned black beans ■ reduced-fat Monterey Jack cheese ■ fresh cilantro ■ lime ■ balsamic vinegar

Looking for a colorful container for my beautiful bean dip, I found myself outside, bringing in the dishes I use when I barbecue. They're plastic, but they look good, don't they? The bowl is deep so I had to make a double recipe, but it wasn't around for long.

Guacamole

The best avocados for guacamole are Haas, the ones with the dark bumpy skin. When properly ripened, they should give slightly when you squeeze, but don't let them ripen too long or they'll be stringy and have black spots inside. Make this as mild or hot as you like by choosing the right chile pepper. For my taste, jalapeños provide just enough of a bite, but if you like to sweat while you eat, try a hotter pepper, like the fiery habanero. Guacamole is best eaten right away, but if you must refrigerate it, bury the avocado pit inside and cover very closely with plastic wrap. This is traditionally served with tortilla chips, but it's also great with crudités, quesadillas, nachos, or as a side to any Mexican dish.

1 Haas avocado

$^1/_4$ cup finely diced jalapeño pepper, seeds removed

$^1/_4$ cup finely diced red onion

1 teaspoon fresh lime juice

$^1/_4$ teaspoon salt

Black pepper to taste

Start-to-Finish
10 minutes

Do I Have What It Takes?
No special equipment is needed.

Shopping List
avocado ▪ jalapeño pepper ▪ red onion ▪ lime

1 Slice the avocado in half, remove the pit, and scoop the flesh into a medium bowl.

2 Add all of the remaining ingredients, and mash with a fork as chunky or smooth as you like.

Health Benefits

Avocados are reported to help reduce the risk of heart disease, hypertension, cancer, high blood pressure, vision loss, diabetes, osteoporosis, and birth defects. The added benefits of the peppers and onions can be anything from thinning the blood and preventing clots, to lowering cholesterol, to improving circulation and memory as well as protecting against asthma and arthritis. Hot chile peppers are reported to increase metabolism to assist in weight loss.

This is the way I like my guacamole—nice and chunky. To create the festive

look in this picture I used a sombrero that's really made to hold salt for margaritas. I

found it at a discount store, and everything else was found around the house.

Mango Salsa

MAKES 2 TO 4 SERVINGS

Pretty much every ingredient in this salsa is a superfood, and what a delicious way to get healthy. To prepare the mango, I peel the whole fruit with a vegetable peeler first, slice down the wide sides, and then cut off the rest in chunks. This colorful and delicious salsa is not just for chip dipping. Pile some on a barbecued chicken breast or grilled fish. How about with scrambled eggs? Or on a burger? Sometimes I just eat it with a spoon. It's best made fresh and served right away.

1 ripe mango, diced

$1/4$ cup diced red onion

2 tablespoons diced jalapeño pepper

2 tablespoons chopped fresh cilantro

2 tablespoons fresh lime juice

$1/8$ teaspoon salt

Black pepper to taste

Start-to-Finish
15 minutes

Do I Have What It Takes?
No special equipment is needed.

Shopping List
mango ▪ red onion ▪ jalapeño pepper ▪ fresh cilantro ▪ lime

In a bowl, combine all of the ingredients, stirring well. Serve immediately.

Health Benefits

If you're concerned about your immune system, cholesterol, eyesight, circulation, and memory, or protecting your lungs and reducing the risk of cancer, this is what to eat.

I can never get two mango salsas to look the same. This one was made from a very

ripe mango and produced a juicier salsa, but a week earlier the mango was firmer and

the salsa was more chunky and less juicy. Two different textures but equally delicious

tastes. The napkin underneath, which I found at Anthropologie, was just perfect for this

tropical fruit dish.

Parmesan Tortilla Crisps

Yes, you can make your own crunchy custom-made chips with less fat than the ones in a bag and a lot more flavor. These are really fun to make, especially when kids can make their own custom chips. I'll give you my favorite chip recipe plus a few other suggestions, but you can always experiment and come up with your own variations. To avoid trans fats, try to find tortillas that do not contain partially hydrogenated fats. They are usually available at health food stores where you can also find some nice whole-grain tortillas.

6 flour tortillas, 7 to 8 inches across

2 tablespoons olive oil

1 large clove garlic

$^1/_4$ cup grated Parmesan cheese

Salt to taste

Start-to-Finish
30 minutes

Do I Have What It Takes?
You'll need two large baking sheets and a basting brush.

Shopping List
flour tortillas ▪ olive oil ▪ garlic ▪ grated Parmesan cheese

1 Preheat the oven to 375°F and set the oven racks in place for 2 baking sheets. Line 2 large baking sheets with parchment paper and set aside.

2 Spread out the tortillas on a work surface and pour the oil into a small bowl. Using a basting brush, lightly coat each tortilla with oil. Cut the garlic clove in half and rub the cut side all over each tortilla. This will also help spread the oil evenly.

3 Sprinkle 2 teaspoons of Parmesan on each tortilla, followed by a very light sprinkling of salt. Cut each tortilla into 8 wedges and transfer to the baking sheets, separating the wedges a bit so they aren't touching.

4 Bake for 8 to 10 minutes or until crisp. Halfway through baking, rotate the baking sheets to the opposite racks so the crisps bake evenly. Store in airtight containers, as if you'll have any left.

Health Benefits

Less fat and fewer calories than store-bought chips.

I was only going to photograph the plain Parmesan crisps but when I experi-

mented with different flavors they turned out so well, I decided to include them

too. Left to right are Pizza Crisps, Parmesan Crisps, and Whole-Grain Parmesan

Crisps, which I made with some sprouted whole-grain tortillas I found at

the health food store.

Here are some other suggestions and combinations:

Cajun Crisps: Olive oil plus Cajun spice mix

Cinnamon Crisps: Rub with a stick of unsalted butter and sprinkle with sugar and cinnamon. Bake for 8 minutes.

Make You Cry: Hot chile oil with Parmesan and cayenne pepper

Pizza Crisps: Tomato paste plus Parmesan and Italian seasoning

Nutty Caramel Corn

MAKES ABOUT 10 CUPS

Don't even try this recipe. It's so good you're liable to eat the entire thing in one sitting and then you'll be packing your bags for a long guilt trip. When you see how easy
it is to make your own crunchy caramel corn maybe you can give some of it away at
Christmastime . . . or not. To pop the corn I suggest using an air popper or a pot on
the stove rather than microwave popcorn, which contains too much junk. White popping corn is my preference over yellow because it's crispier and has fewer hulls. Raw
almonds, walnuts, and pecans can be found in the baking section of the supermarket.
By leaving the nuts on top of the popcorn when you pour the syrup, the nuts are sure
to get glazed all over. And you must bake the corn mixture on a jelly-roll pan with a
rim so the mixture doesn't spill out.

8 cups popped unsalted
popcorn (about a heaping
$^1/_3$ cup popping corn)

$^1/_2$ cup whole raw almonds

$^1/_2$ cup dry roasted lightly
salted peanuts

$^1/_2$ cup whole raw walnuts or
pecans

5 tablespoons unsalted butter

$^1/_4$ cup light corn syrup

$^1/_2$ cup light brown sugar

$^1/_2$ teaspoon salt

$^1/_2$ teaspoon vanilla extract

$^1/_2$ teaspoon baking soda

1   Preheat the oven to 250°F.

2   Discard any unpopped or burned kernels. Into a very large
bowl, place the popped, unsalted popcorn. Spread the
almonds, peanuts, and walnuts or pecans on top of the popcorn but do not mix; leave the nuts resting on top of the popcorn.

3   Into a medium saucepan, place the butter, corn syrup, brown
sugar, and salt. Bring to a boil over medium-low heat, stirring
until the butter is melted. Reduce the heat to low and boil,
undisturbed and uncovered, for 5 minutes. Remove the
saucepan from the heat and stir in the vanilla and baking soda.

4   Immediately pour the butter mixture over the nuts and using
your hands (latex gloves work well here) mix it all up, smoosh-
ing so that all the popcorn and nuts are glazed. This takes a
good minute.

5   Spread the popcorn mixture onto a large ungreased jelly-roll

pan. Mine measures 12 x 17 inches; you can use two smaller pans but they must have rims. Bake for 1 hour, removing briefly every 15 minutes to stir.

6   Spread the mixture onto waxed paper to cool. If you listen closely you'll hear it crackling as it cools. It will seem sticky at first but it will dry up nicely. Store in an airtight container.

Health Benefits

Yes, there really are some benefits to this face-stuffing delight. All of those nuts are full of protein, which helps maintain everything from your brain to your hair and nails. And the omega-3 fatty acids from nuts are reported to protect your heart. Popcorn also provides fiber for a healthy colon.

Start-to-Finish
1 hour and 30 minutes

Do I Have What It Takes?
You'll need a very large bowl and a large jelly-roll pan or two smaller ones. Latex gloves are helpful but not necessary.

Shopping List
popping corn ▪ raw almonds ▪ dry roasted lightly salted peanuts ▪ raw walnuts or pecans ▪ unsalted butter ▪ corn syrup ▪ brown sugar ▪ vanilla ▪ baking soda

People usually snack while they're doing something else, like watching TV, playing board games, or doing a crossword puzzle. That's what made me think of using the paper. The glasses are mine so I can read the puzzle, and the pencil is because I'm not that good.

Thirty-Minute Meals

Broccoli Bean Pasta

MAKES 4 SERVINGS

I make this all the time. It's quick and easy and sooo good for you. Ingredients don't have to be exact and you can substitute other greens, like collards, kale, or mustard greens. If you like your food to bite you back, add some crushed red pepper as the broccoli cooks. When you drain the canned beans, just tip the can over for about 5 seconds, leaving a little juice in the bottom of the can.

$^1/_2$ pound penne pasta

1 bunch rapini, a.k.a. broccoli rabe

1 broccoli crown

1 tablespoon olive oil

1 large clove garlic, minced

2 cups 1% low-fat milk

2 tablespoons all-purpose flour

2 tablespoons grated Parmesan cheese

$^1/_2$ teaspoon salt

Dash of black pepper

Pinch of nutmeg

One 15-ounce can cannellini beans, lightly drained

Start-to-Finish
25 minutes

Do I Have What It Takes?
You'll need a large sauté pan with lid.

1 Cook the pasta according to the package directions.

2 Meanwhile, trim and coarsely chop the rapini, removing any thick stems. Chop the broccoli into bite-size pieces. Wash both vegetables, leaving excess water on them.

3 In a large sauté pan, heat the oil over medium heat. Add the garlic and cook, stirring, for 1 minute, being careful not to let it burn.

4 Add the wet rapini and broccoli to the pan, stirring well. Cover and cook, stirring a couple of times, until softened, about 5 minutes. Add a few tablespoons of pasta water if needed. Remove the broccoli mixture from the pan to a bowl and set aside.

5 In a medium bowl, whisk together the milk and flour and pour into the same sauté pan with the cheese, salt, pepper, and nutmeg. Cook, stirring, until it comes to a boil, then reduce the heat to low. Simmer, stirring, until thickened, 2 to 3 minutes.

6 Add the cooked and drained pasta to sauce first, then add the beans and greens with any juices. Serve with extra Parmesan.

Health Benefits

Broccoli and rapini are reported to protect against birth defects, cataracts, vision loss, and cancer. They also promote strong bones and teeth and support the immune system and cardiovascular health. Beans lower cholesterol, stabilize blood sugar, and suppress the appetite, helping reduce obesity. They may also protect against constipation, diverticulitis, hypertension, type II diabetes, and heart disease.

Shopping List
penne pasta ■ rapini ■ broccoli crown ■ olive oil ■ garlic ■ milk ■ flour ■ grated Parmesan cheese ■ nutmeg ■ canned cannellini beans

This is one of my favorite meals ever and one of my favorite pictures. The table is really a shelf in my living room, the knife and fork are from an antique shop in Sherman Oaks, and the copper mug was five dollars at a secondhand store.

Turkey Chili

Once you chop a few veggies, it's bing, bang, boom, and your chili is done. Chili always tastes better the second day so I usually cook it in the evening and refrigerate it for the next day. Then I freeze leftovers in single servings so there's always something good to eat. This recipe works just as well with regular ground turkey or beef, but turkey breast is the leanest. If you don't have diced tomatoes, you can use canned whole, crushed, or even tomato sauce—whatever you have around. I prefer to use crushed or diced so there are no big chunks. It's hard to ruin a chili recipe, so feel free to make this your own by adding extra hot chiles, hot sauce, or even a jar of salsa. You can even throw in some beer. Masa flour is made from corn and available in most supermarkets.

1 tablespoon olive oil

1 cup diced onion

2 cloves garlic, minced

1 cup diced red bell pepper

$^1/_3$ cup diced jalapeño pepper

1 pound ground turkey breast

1$^1/_2$ cups chicken or vegetable stock, or water

1 cup canned crushed tomatoes with added puree

One 15-ounce can dark red kidney beans, lightly drained

$^1/_4$ cup chopped fresh parsley

1 tablespoon chili powder

1 bay leaf

1 teaspoon salt

Black pepper to taste

2 tablespoons masa flour or regular flour

$^1/_4$ cup water

1. In a large pot, heat the oil over medium heat. Add the onion and garlic and cook, stirring, until the onion is translucent, about 2 minutes. Add the bell pepper and jalapeño and cook, stirring, for another 2 minutes.

2. Add the turkey to the pot, stirring to break it up, and cook, stirring, until it's no longer pink, about 3 minutes. Add the stock or water, tomatoes, beans, parsley, chili powder, bay leaf, salt, and pepper. Bring to a boil, then reduce heat, cover, and cook at a gentle boil for 15 minutes.

3. In a small bowl, whisk the masa flour with the water and stir into the chili. Cook another 5 minutes to thicken.

Kitchen Tip

Peeling Garlic

Lay something flat like a wide knife or spatula or even a piece of cardboard on the clove of garlic. Smack it hard. The peel comes right off.

Health Benefits

Beans are proven to lower cholesterol and are recommended for diabetics because they help keep blood sugar levels stabilized. They may also protect against heart disease, cancer, high blood pressure, and osteoporosis. The healthy assortment of vegetables here may protect you against cancer, heart disease, macular degeneration, cataracts, blood clots, memory loss, and even wrinkles. And the hotter the chile peppers, the better for your blood pressure, and the more fat you will burn.

Start-to-Finish
30 minutes

Do I Have What It Takes?
A large Dutch oven or soup pot with a lid is all you need.

Shopping List
olive oil ▪ onion ▪ garlic ▪ red bell pepper ▪ jalapeño pepper ▪ ground turkey ▪ chicken or vegetable stock (optional) ▪ canned crushed tomatoes with added puree ▪ canned red kidney beans ▪ fresh parsley ▪ chili powder ▪ bay leaf ▪ masa or regular flour

I swear I can smell this fragrant chili right off the page. The purple fabric was too purple for me so I put a layer of red netting on it, and then crumpled up more red netting for the background. I thought the rich colors were a perfect fit for my rich and hearty chili.

Chicken and Peppers MAKES 4 TO 6 SERVINGS

It's 30 minutes from start to finish once your ingredients are ready. Using homemade chicken stock puts this dish into flavor overdrive, and you can use chicken breast or chicken tenders, which are just what they say . . . tender. A variety of colored peppers gives you the most health benefits. This is a big mountain of peppers so you'll need a good-size pan with tall sides and a lid. Mine measures 11 inches across the top.

2 teaspoons olive oil

$^3/_4$ pound boneless chicken breast, cut into 1-inch chunks

$^3/_4$ teaspoon salt

Black pepper to taste

$^1/_2$ cup diced onion

1 clove garlic, minced

1$^1/_2$ cups long-grain rice

1 tablespoon tomato paste

$^1/_4$ teaspoon dried thyme leaves

2$^1/_2$ cups chicken or vegetable stock or water

3 bell peppers (red, yellow, orange, or green), cut into $^1/_2$-inch-wide strips

2 tablespoons chopped fresh parsley

Start-to-Finish
30 minutes plus 10 minutes resting time

Do I Have What It Takes?
You'll need a large sauté pan with a lid.

1   In a large sauté pan, heat 1 teaspoon of the olive oil over medium heat. Add chicken pieces and sprinkle with $^1/_4$ teaspoon of the salt and a little pepper. Cook, stirring, just to brown all sides for 3 or 4 minutes, but do not cook through. Remove the chicken to a bowl.

2   In the same pan, heat the remaining 1 teaspoon olive oil over medium heat. Add the onion and garlic and cook, stirring, for 1 minute. Add the rice, tomato paste, and thyme and cook, stirring, for 2 minutes.

3   Add the stock or water, bell pepper strips, parsley, chicken with its juices, the remaining $^1/_2$ teaspoon of salt, and pepper. Combine thoroughly, bring to a boil, then reduce the heat to low, cover, and cook for 20 minutes, stirring occasionally.

4   Remove from heat and let stand, covered, for 10 minutes so all the liquid gets absorbed.

Kitchen Tip
Handling Raw Poultry

I always keep a box of latex gloves in my kitchen. You can get a box of 100 at the beauty supply. Put them on to handle raw poultry, mix meat loaf, or do any messy kitchen job. Toss the gloves and your hands are bacteria-free.

Health Benefits

These multicolored peppers can protect against cancer, heart disease, macular degeneration, and memory loss, as well as boost your immune system and support your urinary tract. They are also recommended for those with arthritis and asthma. The lean chicken provides high-quality protein, which is essential for healthy growth and development as well as a properly functioning metabolism. Protein supports your muscles, blood, heart, brain, and more. Think of protein as the building superintendent of your body.

Shopping List

olive oil ▪ boneless chicken breast ▪ onion ▪ garlic ▪ long-grain rice ▪ tomato paste ▪ dried thyme leaves ▪ chicken or vegetable stock (optional) ▪ bell peppers ▪ fresh parsley

This is my most used pan because I love to prepare one-dish meals. It's resting on one of my kitchen towels from Bed Bath & Beyond, and that's resting on my breakfast table, which is actually my "eat-all-my-meals-at" table. When I say "sauté pan" this is what I mean.

Chicken Asparagus Bow Ties

MAKES 4 SERVINGS

This is so creamy and comfy, you'll swear it's fettuccine Alfredo. Except for the pasta, everything cooks in one pan so it's best to use a big one with high sides. The chicken should be cut into bite-size pieces. Don't overcook the chicken or it will be tough. For the asparagus, bend it near the bottom of the stalk until the lowest part snaps off. If it's thick you should peel the stalk, but there's no need to peel the slender ones.

8 ounces bow-tie pasta

3 teaspoons olive oil

1 pound boneless chicken breast, cut into 1-inch chunks

1/2 teaspoon salt

1 bunch asparagus, cut into 1-inch pieces (about 2 cups)

1 tablespoon unsalted butter

1 tablespoon all-purpose flour

1 1/2 cups 1% low-fat milk

1/4 cup grated Parmesan cheese

Black pepper to taste

Start-to-Finish
30 minutes

Do I Have What It Takes?
You just need a large sauté pan.

1 Cook the pasta as per the package directions.

2 While the pasta cooks, in a large sauté pan, heat 2 teaspoons of the oil over medium heat. Add the chicken, sprinkle with 1/4 teaspoon of the salt, and cook, stirring, until nicely browned on all sides and cooked through, about 5 minutes. Remove the chicken to a bowl and set aside. I always line the bowl with foil to save washing a dish, plus it keeps the chicken warm.

3 In the same pan, heat the remaining 1 teaspoon of oil over medium heat and add the asparagus. Cook, stirring, until softened but not soggy, 3 to 4 minutes. Remove the asparagus to the bowl with the chicken.

4 Remove the pan from the heat to cool it down a little, then add the butter and place the pan over medium-low heat. Add the flour and stir with a whisk for about a minute. While whisking, slowly add the milk and bring to a boil. Continue cooking, stirring, until thickened, about 3 minutes.

5 Remove the pan from the heat and stir in the Parmesan, bow ties, the remaining 1/4 teaspoon of salt, and pepper. Stir in the chicken and asparagus with any juices that remain.

Health Benefits

The high-quality protein from the chicken is essential for healthy skin, hair, nails, heart, and brain, as well as your metabolism. Asparagus may protect you from heart disease and cancer and prevent birth defects.

Shopping List
bow-tie pasta ▪ olive oil ▪ boneless chicken breast ▪ asparagus ▪ unsalted butter ▪ flour ▪ milk ▪ grated Parmesan cheese

Doesn't this look rich and fattening? Well it's not. In this photo I really wanted to show the comfy creaminess of this dish. The place mat came from the mall and the bamboo-style fork was fifty cents at a Goodwill store.

Salmon Patties   MAKES 2 TO 4 SERVINGS

Running low on groceries? As long as you keep some canned salmon around, there's always something to eat. Having grown up in Canada, I've been eating salmon sandwiches all my life. When Canadians ask, "Do you want that on white or brown?" I always say brown. Little did I know then how important fish was in the diet. I often make salmon sandwiches for lunch (just like tuna, it's mixed with mayo), but if it's suppertime I love these high-protein salmon patties, especially with my Spaghetti with Greens (see page 132) on the side. They also go great with a baked sweet potato. Canned salmon bones are soft and mashable and are an excellent source of calcium, so be sure not to throw them away. But you knew that, eh?

One 7.5-ounce can red salmon, drained

$^1/_4$ cup finely diced onion

$^1/_4$ cup finely diced red bell pepper

1 tablespoon chopped fresh parsley

1 large egg

$^1/_3$ cup oat bran

1 teaspoon olive oil

Start-to-Finish
15 minutes

Do I Have What It Takes?
No special equipment is needed.

Shopping List
canned red salmon ▪ onion ▪ red bell pepper ▪ fresh parsley ▪ egg ▪ oat bran ▪ olive oil

1   In a medium bowl, place the drained salmon and remove any large sections of fatty skin. Mash the salmon with a fork, and be sure to include the bones. Add the onion, bell pepper, parsley, egg, and oat bran and mix well. Shape into four 4-inch patties.

2   In a medium skillet, heat the oil over medium-high heat. Add the patties and cook until nicely browned, about 3 minutes per side.

Health Benefits

The omega-3 fatty acids in the salmon can boost your immune system and protect against coronary artery disease, hypertension, macular degeneration, arthritis, and possibly even depression. Salmon might also give you shiny hair, better skin, and stronger nails. Oat bran lowers cholesterol and red bell pepper can protect your eyes and heart and may help reduce the risk of cancer.

I just realized that the green plate matches the parsley in the patties. This place mat from Pier One reminded me of a harbor dock, which reminded me of fish, so here it is. The trick in this photo was to get the light on the patties but not reflecting off the plate.

Black Bean Quesadilla

MAKES 1 OR 2 SERVINGS PER QUESADILLA

Starving and can't wait? Low blood sugar? This is faster than looking up the number for Domino's. The best pan to use is a crepe pan or one with slightly curved sides so you can slide this baby out when it's done. You can even slide it out onto a plate to help turn it over while cooking instead of using a spatula. The only tortillas I can find that do not contain partially hydrogenated fats are in the health food store. Monterey Jack cheese is my favorite but pepper Jack cheese would be good for all you hotties out there. Remember that canned chiles come in mild and hot versions.

FOR EACH QUESADILLA YOU'LL NEED

¹/₂ cup shredded reduced-fat Monterey Jack cheese

¹/₂ cup canned black beans, drained

¹/₄ cup canned diced green chiles

2 flour tortillas

Canola or olive oil, for greasing pan

Start-to-Finish
15 minutes

Do I Have What It Takes?
No special equipment is needed.

Shopping List
reduced-fat Monterey Jack cheese ▪ canned black beans ▪ canned diced green chiles ▪ flour tortillas ▪ oil

1 Spread the cheese, beans, and chiles on 1 tortilla and top with the other.

2 Preheat a nonstick skillet over medium-low heat and brush with a little oil. Place the quesadilla in the skillet and cook until the cheese starts to melt, about 5 minutes. Flip the quesadilla over by using a large spatula or just slide it onto a dinner plate, cover with another plate, turn it over, and slide it back onto the pan. Cook for another 4 to 5 minutes. Remove to a plate and cut into serving wedges.

Health Benefits

Beans are known to lower cholesterol levels and to stabilize blood sugar. They may help prevent heart disease, diabetes, and cancer. The hotter the chile peppers, the more protection you may be getting from blood clots, heart disease, arthritis, and asthma. Chile peppers boost your metabolism to help burn fat. Both the beans and cheese are high in calcium for strong bones.

I picked up this vibrant plate at a department store and placed it on a piece

of fabric I bought on sale. The green mug in the back is one of those frosty mugs that

you freeze and then it keeps your drink cold.

Rainbow Fried Rice

MAKES 3 TO 4 SERVINGS

Feeling guilty about that pizza you had last night? Couldn't stop at one scoop of ice cream? I should have called this "Morning After" Fried Rice because it will ease your conscience for all those banned substances you sent down to your stomach the night before. It's easy to digest, full of antioxidants, and oh, so good. Whenever I make this, there is not one morsel left in the pan. I think your body knows when it's getting something good. This is basically a stir-fry so be sure to have everything chopped and ready in advance. Once you start you really have to keep stirring until it's done. The rice can be cooked in advance and refrigerated. Otherwise, put the rice on before you start prepping your vegetables.

I cup uncooked long-grain rice

I teaspoon canola oil

I clove garlic, minced

$^1/_3$ cup each of diced:

  red onion

  celery

  red bell pepper

  yellow bell pepper

  orange bell pepper

  green bell pepper

$^1/_3$ cup shredded carrot

I cup chopped bok choy leaves

2 large eggs, lightly beaten

I teaspoon low-sodium soy sauce

$^1/_4$ teaspoon salt

Black pepper to taste

I green onion (scallion), chopped

1   Cook the rice as per the package directions.

2   Meanwhile, in a large sauté pan, heat the oil over medium heat. Add the garlic, onion, and celery and cook, stirring, for 1 minute. Add the red, yellow, orange, and green bell peppers, carrot, and bok choy and cook, stirring, for 3 minutes. Add the cooked rice and stir for 1 minute more.

3   Reduce the heat to low, push the rice mixture to one side of the pan, and add the eggs. Scramble them for a minute, then stir into the rice.

4   Sprinkle with the soy sauce, salt, and pepper and stir well. Serve topped with green onions.

Health Benefits

When you eat this many immune-boosting vibrant colors the list of possible benefits includes protection against heart disease, cancer, asthma, arthritis, osteoporosis, macular degeneration, and blood clots. You may also have improved circulation, blood pressure, cholesterol levels, and memory. Plus, peppers help you burn fat.

Start-to-Finish
30 minutes

Do I Have What It Takes?
You'll need a very large sauté pan or wok.

Shopping List
long-grain rice ▪ canola oil ▪ garlic ▪ red onion ▪ celery ▪ red, yellow, orange, and green bell peppers ▪ carrot ▪ bok choy ▪ eggs ▪ low-sodium soy sauce ▪ green onion (scallion)

It may look like a kitchen tablecloth but that's just a piece of plaid fabric.

The chopsticks were a souvenir from dinner at Benihana and the curly bowl

came from a discount store. But the best thing in this picture is definitely the cacophony

of colors in my Rainbow Fried Rice.

Super Suppers

Mac and Cheese
MAKES 6 TO 8 SERVINGS

I won't lie and tell you this dish is easy, but I will tell you it's worth the effort and it's a low-fat version you're gonna love. Tomatoes make a great partner to mac and cheese, and their health benefits are the perfect excuse to enjoy what I believe is the ultimate comfort food. Use any shape pasta you like but I think the squiggly kind, like rotelle or large elbows, are best. Just be sure to undercook the pasta by about a minute. Try to use one solid piece of onion in the sauce for easy retrieval. Now I know they sell lots of preshredded cheeses but shredding your own makes a better sauce. This cheesy pasta goes great with a side of steamed broccoli. To make fresh bread crumbs, put 2 slices of white bread (no crusts) in a food processor and spin for about 30 seconds.

12 ounces elbows or other pasta (about 4 cups)

2^{1}/$_{2}$ cups 1% low-fat milk

^{1}/$_{4}$ cup flour

2-inch wedge of onion

1 clove garlic, halved

1 bay leaf

8 ounces reduced-fat sharp cheddar cheese, shredded or thin sliced

1 tablespoon grated Parmesan cheese

^{1}/$_{2}$ teaspoon salt

Black pepper to taste

2 large tomatoes, diced and seeded

1 cup fresh bread crumbs plus 1 tablespoon grated Parmesan cheese, for topping

1 Preheat the oven to 375°F. Lightly butter a 3-quart casserole dish.

2 Cook the pasta for about 1 minute less than package directions specify.

3 In a large bowl, whisk together the milk and flour. In a large sauté pan, place the milk and flour mixture along with the onion, garlic, and bay leaf. Bring to a boil over medium-high heat, stirring a few times with a whisk. Reduce the heat to low and cook at a gentle boil, stirring a few times, until thickened, about 10 minutes.

4 Remove the pan from the heat. Using a slotted spoon, remove the onion, garlic, and bay leaf. Add the cheddar cheese, Parmesan, salt, and pepper and stir until well blended.

5 Add the cooked and drained pasta and the tomatoes to the cheese sauce and pour everything into the casserole dish.

6 Sprinkle the bread crumbs and grated Parmesan cheese over the top and bake, uncovered, for 20 to 25 minutes until the top is golden.

Health Benefits

Cheese provides calcium for strong bones and to help against hypertension. Tomatoes are believed to protect against heart disease, macular degeneration, and cancer, particularly prostate cancer. Tomatoes may also support a healthy urinary tract and prevent memory loss and even wrinkles.

I went all out for this picture because hey, it's mac and cheese! Who can live without it? I was a shopping fool at the Fiesta store because I thought an old-fashioned homey look for this old-fashioned homey dish was perfect.

Start-to-Finish
1 hour

Do I Have What It Takes?
You'll need a 3-quart baking dish, your biggest sauté pan, and a hand or box grater for the cheese.

Shopping List
elbows or other pasta ▪ milk ▪ flour ▪ onion ▪ garlic ▪ bay leaf ▪ reduced fat sharp cheddar cheese ▪ grated Parmesan cheese ▪ tomatoes ▪ fresh bread crumbs or slices of bread to make fresh

Only the best for my all-time favorite comfort food!

Meat Loaf

MAKES 4 TO 6 SERVINGS

Who ever thought that old-fashioned meat loaf could provide so many health benefits? They don't all do but mine does. All these multicolored veggies add flavor **AND** many antiaging benefits. And what's better than some leftover meat loaf, sliced on a sourdough roll for sandwich heaven? I always see meat loaf mixes containing beef, pork, and other meats, but you'll get less saturated fat using the leanest beef you can. If you make this and don't cook up some real mashed potatoes to go with it . . . then suffer in silence. I make my fluffy mashed potatoes with just some buttermilk, salt, and pepper. Yummm.

1 teaspoon olive oil

$1/2$ cup chopped onion

2 cloves garlic, minced

$1/4$ teaspoon dried thyme leaves

$1/2$ cup quick-cooking oats

$1/3$ cup 1% low-fat milk

$1/4$ cup finely chopped red bell pepper

$1/4$ cup finely chopped green bell pepper

$1/4$ cup shredded carrot

$1/2$ cup ketchup

1 large egg

$1/4$ cup chopped fresh parsley

1 teaspoon Dijon mustard

$1/2$ teaspoon salt

Black pepper to taste

$1 1/2$ pounds extra-lean ground beef

1   Preheat the oven to 350°F. Line a baking sheet with foil and set aside.

2   In a small fry pan, heat the oil over medium-low heat. Add the onion, garlic, and thyme and cook, stirring, until the onion is translucent, about 5 minutes. Set aside to cool.

3   In a large bowl, combine the cooled onion mixture with the remaining ingredients, except for the meat. When the mixture is well blended, add the meat by hand but do not overwork it.

4   Place the meat mixture on the baking sheet and shape into a 9 x 5-inch loaf. Bake for about 1 hour or until the center reaches 160°F on a meat thermometer inserted in the middle. Let rest for 10 minutes before serving.

Kitchen Tip

Garlic Breath?

Chew on some fresh parsley. It contains chlorophyll.

Health Benefits

Lean meat is an excellent source of protein, which we need for the development and repair of tissues and the maintenance of muscles, including the brain. Beef provides heme iron, a much more absorbable iron for anyone who is deficient. Protein benefits your hair, skin, and nails as well as your metabolism. The oats provide soluble fiber, which is known to reduce cholesterol levels and stabilize blood sugar. The vegetables may protect you from heart disease and cancer and support your eye health, cholesterol, and blood pressure.

Start-to-Finish
1 hour and 15 minutes plus 10 minutes resting time

Do I Have What It Takes?
All you need is a baking sheet.

Shopping List
olive oil ▪ onion ▪ garlic ▪ dried thyme leaves ▪ quick-cooking oats ▪ milk ▪ red and green bell peppers ▪ carrot ▪ ketchup ▪ egg ▪ fresh parsley ▪ Dijon mustard ▪ ground beef

Can you spot the item in this picture that has my name on it? No, it's not the meat loaf although yes, I did eat it right after taking the photo. It's the mug in the

background that has my name etched on it.

Stuffed Peppers MAKES 8 SERVINGS

A stuffed pepper is a meal in itself and so pretty to serve when you have several colors. Varying the colors provides the broadest range of antioxidant benefits as well. You can either steam the peppers in a pot with a steamer basket or microwave them with a little water for a couple of minutes to soften.

1 teaspoon olive oil

$^1/_2$ cup chopped onion

1 clove garlic, minced

$^1/_2$ cup sliced almonds

1 cup finely chopped mushrooms

$^3/_4$ cup uncooked long-grain rice

1$^1/_2$ cups hot chicken or vegetable stock, or water

2 tablespoons chopped fresh parsley

$^1/_2$ teaspoon salt

Black pepper to taste

4 bell peppers (red, yellow, orange, and green)

Start-to-Finish
1 hour and 15 minutes

Do I Have What It Takes?
You'll need a 13 x 9-inch baking dish and aluminum foil. A steamer basket is helpful but not required.

1 Preheat the oven to 375°F.

2 In a large sauté pan, heat the oil over medium heat. Add the onion and garlic and cook, stirring often, until the onion is translucent, 2 to 3 minutes. Add the almonds, mushrooms, and rice and cook, stirring, for another 2 minutes.

3 Add the hot stock, parsley, salt, and pepper, bring to a boil, then reduce the heat, cover, and simmer for 20 minutes.

4 While the rice cooks, core the peppers and cut each in half lengthwise, discarding the seeds and white membrane. Using a steamer basket over simmering water in a large pot, steam the peppers for about 5 minutes to soften.

5 When the rice is done, remove from the heat and let it stand, covered, for 10 minutes to absorb all the liquid. Meanwhile, put a quart of water on to boil.

6 Place the peppers in a 13 x 9-inch baking dish, and fill each with the rice mixture. Pour $^1/_4$ inch of boiling water around the peppers, cover the pan with foil, and bake for 30 minutes.

Kitchen Tip

Never Store Mushrooms in a Plastic Bag

They will get soggy. Keep them refrigerated, but exposed to air.

Health Benefits

All these beautifully colored peppers can protect against cancer, heart disease, macular degeneration, and memory loss. They can boost your immune system and strengthen your urinary tract. Peppers are also reported to help burn fat for increased weight loss, and are recommended for those with arthritis and asthma. Mushrooms are immunity-boosters, and almonds may protect against heart disease, high cholesterol, and Alzheimer's as well as improve your skin.

Shopping List

olive oil ▪ onion ▪ garlic ▪ sliced almonds ▪ mushrooms ▪ long-grain rice ▪ chicken or vegetable stock (optional) ▪ fresh parsley ▪ red, yellow, orange, and green bell peppers

It was hard to go wrong photographing these beautiful and vivid peppers. This is one of the first photos I took and I bought a deep red piece of fabric just for this shot. The long blue bowl came from a secondhand store and hugged the peppers perfectly.

Chicken-Vegetable Stew

MAKES 4 TO 6 SERVINGS

Stew does not have to cook for hours. In fact, peeling your vegetables may take longer than cooking them, but it is important to have everything ready before you start because this dish comes together quickly. However, don't combine your stock and flour until just before needing it, otherwise it gets a bit sticky. I included broccoli in this stew because it's such an important antioxidant-packed vegetable, and I try to eat it as often as possible. For me, this dish screams for a hunk of crusty sourdough bread for dunking.

1 teaspoon olive oil

1 pound boneless chicken breast, cut into 1-inch chunks

Pinch plus $1/2$ teaspoon salt

Black pepper to taste

1 cup chopped onion

2 cloves garlic, minced

$2^1/2$ cups chicken stock

$1/3$ cup all-purpose flour

1 large carrot, cut into 1-inch slices

1 stalk celery, cut into 1-inch slices

1 small rutabaga, cut into 1-inch pieces

10 to 12 small red potatoes, halved (unless they're really tiny)

10 to 12 tiny mushrooms (halved if large)

1 bay leaf

1 cup small broccoli florets

$1/4$ cup chopped fresh parsley

1 In a large sauté pan, heat the oil over medium-high heat. Add the chicken, sprinkle with a pinch of salt and pepper, and cook, turning and separating, until all sides are lightly browned, 2 to 3 minutes. Add the onion and garlic and cook, stirring, for 1 minute more.

2 In a small bowl, whisk together the chicken stock and flour and add to the pan. Add the carrot, celery, rutabaga, potatoes, mushrooms, bay leaf, $1/2$ teaspoon salt, and some pepper. Bring to a boil, then reduce the heat to low, cover, and cook for 15 minutes.

3 Stir in the broccoli and parsley, cover, and cook for another 3 minutes. All done.

Health Benefits

Besides the high-quality protein from the chicken, which you need for everything from a healthy brain to beautiful skin, hair, and nails, all these immunity-boosting vegetables can help protect you from cancer, cardiovascular disease, memory loss, and macular degeneration.

Start-to-Finish
50 minutes

Do I Have What It Takes?
You'll need a large sauté pan with a lid.

Shopping List
olive oil ▪ chicken breast ▪ onion ▪ garlic ▪ chicken stock ▪ flour ▪ carrot ▪ celery ▪ rutabaga ▪ red potatoes ▪ mushrooms ▪ bay leaf ▪ broccoli ▪ fresh parsley

In trying to show every aspect of this scrumptious stew, I realize now that I may have overloaded the bowl just a little. I just wanted you to see everything. The white bowl is from my everyday dishes, and I bought the place mat on sale.

Tortilla Pie   MAKES 4 TO 6 SERVINGS

You can make this layered pie as hot as you want with your choice of chile pepper and salsa. I used a mild Anaheim chile, but you can go a little hotter with a jalapeño, and hotter still with a serrano. If you don't have a round casserole dish, use a pie plate lined with foil that extends 6 inches over the edges. Then use the foil to cover it before baking. Look for tortillas that do not contain partially hydrogenated oils. I can only find them at the health food store. And I know it's easy to buy preshredded cheese, but it won't be as good as shredding your own.

1 teaspoon olive oil

$^1/_2$ cup chopped red onion

1 clove garlic, minced

$^1/_2$ cup chopped red bell pepper

$^1/_2$ cup chopped green bell pepper

$^1/_2$ cup chopped Anaheim pepper (or a hotter chile pepper)

One 15-ounce can black beans, lightly drained

One 15-ounce can cannellini beans, lightly drained

1 cup bottled thick and chunky salsa, mild or hot

1 tablespoon chopped fresh cilantro

Six 8-inch flour tortillas

6 ounces shredded reduced-fat Jack cheese (1$^1/_2$ cups)

1   Preheat the oven to 325°F. Lightly grease the bottom and sides of an 8-inch round casserole dish with butter.

2   In a large sauté pan, heat the oil over medium heat. Add the onion and garlic and cook, stirring, until the onion is just translucent, about 2 minutes. Add the red and green bell peppers and the Anaheim pepper and cook, stirring, until the peppers are slightly softened, 2 to 3 minutes. Add the black and cannellini beans, salsa, and cilantro and cook just to blend the flavors, 2 to 3 minutes.

3   Layer the ingredients in the casserole dish in this order: 1 tortilla, then $^2/_3$ cup bean mixture and $^1/_4$ cup cheese. Repeat with the remaining tortillas, ending with the beans and cheese.

4   Cover and bake for 30 minutes. Serve alone or with extra salsa or sour cream (both optional).

Health Benefits

Beans are known to lower cholesterol, which can protect you against heart disease. They also provide calcium to help prevent osteoporosis (as does the cheese). Beans are believed to help protect against cancer and are recommended for diabetics because they help keep blood sugar regulated. Their protein is essential to good health and may also improve your hair, nails, and skin. The multicolored peppers may support your eye health, lungs, joints, and heart and may reduce the risk of cancer. Chile peppers increase your metabolism to burn more fat and thin the blood to help prevent clots. The onions and salsa can also thin the blood, protect the heart and eyes, strengthen capillaries, improve memory, and may protect against cancer.

Start-to-Finish
I hour

Do I Have What It Takes?
You'll need an 8-inch round casserole with lid (or a pie pan with foil will work) plus a shredder or box grater to shred the cheese.

Shopping List
olive oil ▪ red onion ▪ garlic ▪ red bell pepper ▪ green bell pepper ▪ chile pepper (Anaheim or hotter) ▪ canned black beans ▪ canned cannellini beans ▪ bottled salsa ▪ fresh cilantro ▪ flour tortillas ▪ reduced-fat Jack cheese

I had gotten these dishes a few years ago at Marshall Field's in Chicago and

how perfect are they for my tortilla pie? I paired this plate with a hand-painted

pitcher and goblet I picked up at a craft fair and the turquoise

napkin wasn't really a napkin, just a folded piece of fabric.

Fish and Chips   MAKES 4 SERVINGS

Everybody loves fish 'n' chips, but the fried version is just so unhealthy. Try to buy the fish the day it comes in to the market, and it helps if the fish is the same thickness through-out so it cooks evenly. Even though it's filleted, give your fish the once-over for bones. You will probably find some and they must go! I recommend latex or rubber gloves for handling and breading the fish, and I do everything on a long sheet of waxed paper for effortless cleanup. Get the "chips" in the oven first, then prepare the fish. The easiest way to fine-chop the almonds is to run them in the food processor for about 30 seconds.

CHIPS

1 1/2 pounds russet potatoes

2 tablespoons olive oil

1/4 teaspoon salt

1/4 teaspoon seasoned salt (optional)

Black pepper to taste

FISH

1/4 cup yellow or white cornmeal

1/2 cup plain bread crumbs

2 tablespoons very finely chopped almonds (12 almonds)

2 tablespoons chopped fresh parsley

1/4 teaspoon salt

Black pepper to taste

2 large egg whites

1 pound filet of cod, cut into 4 pieces

1 Preheat the oven to 475°F. Lightly coat a large baking sheet with olive oil.

2 Peel and cut the potatoes into 3/8 -inch strips and pat dry using paper towels. Toss with the oil, salt, seasoned salt (if using), and pepper. The easiest way to do this is to put the oil, salt, and pepper into a plastic bag and then add the sliced potatoes. You can shake, squeeze, and smoosh until the potatoes are coated.

3 Spread the potatoes on the baking sheet and bake for 25 min-utes. After 15 minutes stir and turn over the potatoes with a spatula and continue baking. Meanwhile, prepare the fish.

4 Spread out a long sheet of waxed paper to work on and place the cornmeal at one end. At the other end combine the bread crumbs, almonds, parsley, salt, and pepper.

5 Place the egg whites in a shallow bowl and stir lightly with a fork. Dip each piece of fish in cornmeal, then in the egg whites, then coat with the crumb mixture, and place on an oven-safe metal rack.

6 After the potatoes have roasted for 25 minutes, remove them from the oven. Turn the potatoes again with a spatula and place the rack with the fish directly on top of the potatoes.

Return everything to the oven and bake for 15 minutes until the fish is crisp and golden.

Health Benefits

Fish is important for heart health. It can help keep your cholesterol and triglycerides in check, as well as your blood pressure. It can also help with arthritis, hypertension, and depression, plus it's good for your hair, skin, and nails. Potatoes are a good source of potassium, which may help with blood pressure, heart health, and stroke prevention.

Start-to-Finish
50 minutes

Do I Have What It Takes?
You'll need a large baking sheet and an oven-safe metal rack.

Shopping List
potatoes ▪ olive oil ▪ seasoned salt (optional) ▪ cornmeal ▪ bread crumbs ▪ almonds ▪ fresh parsley ▪ eggs ▪ fresh cod

A piece of yellow burlap, an old plaid kitchen towel, a discounted glass plate, and my fish 'n' chips look pretty good, don't they? That's actually tartar sauce in the bowl behind and the bigger glass bowl has extra potatoes.

Pasta, Rice, and Grains

Spaghetti with Greens

This is one of my favorite recipes in the book. It's a delicious way to get those important greens, and it makes a great side dish for some grilled chicken or my Salmon Patties (see page 110). You can substitute other greens like collards or spinach, but I would not use kale because it's a little too coarse. If the final dish seems too dry, just add a little extra olive oil. I like to serve this with extra Parmesan for sprinkling.

8 ounces spaghetti

1 bunch Swiss chard

1 teaspoon olive oil, plus 2 tablespoons for serving

1 clove garlic, minced

2 tablespoons water

$1/4$ teaspoon salt

Black pepper to taste

2 teaspoons grated Parmesan cheese

Start-to-Finish
20 minutes

Do I Have What It Takes?
No special equipment is needed.

Shopping List
spaghetti ▪ chard ▪ olive oil ▪ garlic ▪ grated Parmesan cheese

1   Cook the spaghetti as per package directions.

2   Meanwhile, trim the chard by removing any thick ribs and cut the leafy green parts into large chunks or strips. Wash well and leave it wet.

3   In a large sauté pan, heat the 1 teaspoon olive oil over medium heat. Add the garlic and cook, stirring, until lightly golden, about 1 minute, being careful not to let it burn. Stir in the wet greens and cook, stirring, for a minute or two, until the greens are soft and wilted.

4   Add the water (you can use some hot pasta water here), salt, and pepper. Reduce the heat to medium-low and continue to cook, stirring, for 3 or 4 minutes. Remove the pan from the heat, cover, and set aside until the pasta is done.

5   Add the cooked and drained spaghetti to the greens. Stir in the extra 2 tablespoons of olive oil and the Parmesan and serve.

Health Benefits

Greens can provide protection against breast, prostate, lung, and other cancers, high cholesterol, and vision loss. They can protect your bones and teeth and boost your immune system. Olive oil and garlic may protect the heart. Garlic may also thin the blood to help prevent clots, and help fight infections, memory loss, and cancer.

The plate and round saltshaker are from a store that sells Fiestaware. The

"tablecloth" was a half yard of fabric I purchased, and I got really lucky

when I found this beautifully colored Swiss chard at Whole Foods. This whole plate was

eaten and gone in five minutes. I love it!

Spinach Pesto

Here's an easy and delicious way to get some of that superfood called spinach into your diet. You can't buy pesto sauce that tastes this good in any store. All you really need is a food processor to make this, and it takes only minutes. Use more garlic if you want to—in fact use as much as you can stand—and adjust the salt and pepper according to your taste. There are lots of things to do with pesto sauce besides just stirring it into hot pasta (which is why it's in this chapter): use it on sandwiches or steamed vegetables, serve it with chicken, or coat some fish with it before cooking. Whatever you choose, you'll know that you're doing your body a lot of good.

2 cups baby spinach leaves, lightly packed

$1/2$ cup fresh basil leaves, lightly packed

I clove garlic

2 tablespoons pine nuts

2 tablespoons grated Parmesan cheese

$1/4$ cup olive oil

$1/4$ teaspoon salt

Black pepper to taste

Start-to-Finish
5 minutes

Do I Have What It Takes?
You'll need a food processor.

Shopping List
fresh baby spinach ▪ fresh basil ▪ garlic ▪ pine nuts ▪ grated Parmesan cheese ▪ olive oil

Into a food processor fitted with the metal blade, place the spinach, basil, garlic, pine nuts, and Parmesan. Process while slowly adding olive oil—this takes about 30 seconds. Scrape down the sides of the bowl and process another few seconds. Add salt and pepper to taste. Refrigerate until ready to use.

Health Benefits

Spinach does it all. It can protect you from cancer, heart disease, stroke, macular degeneration, and cataracts. They also call it brain food because it may slow the aging of your brain. Garlic has antibiotic properties and may thin the blood to help prevent clots, improve circulation and memory, and may also reduce the risk of heart disease and cancer.

Picture this if you can. I'm alone working on this photo and decide that this fabulous curly

spaghetti would look great being picked up with two forks, just like you would to serve it.

There is a large lamp on my left, which needs to stay there to light the dish, so if I use my

left hand to hold the forks it casts a shadow. I'm right-handed and had to improvise. So I

set the camera on auto-focus, held it in my contorted left hand, held the forks with my right

and snapped. I was shocked to get the photo, but here it is.

Broccoli Rice

MAKES 6 TO 8 SERVINGS

Look up "easy" in the dictionary and you'll see a picture of this dish (right next to my cousin's friend, Misty, but that's another book). To make this side dish even tastier, use chicken or vegetable stock to cook the rice. Have the broccoli ready in a bowl and toss it in quickly so the lid goes right back on and the rice keeps cooking. There is no need to stir it in. This is a tasty way to get one of the most important vegetables on the planet.

1 cup long-grain rice

3 cups broccoli florets

1 tablespoon grated Parmesan cheese

1 tablespoon fresh lemon juice

$1/4$ teaspoon salt

Black pepper to taste

Start-to-Finish
25 minutes

Do I Have What It Takes?
No special equipment is needed.

Shopping List
long-grain rice ▪ broccoli ▪ grated Parmesan cheese ▪ lemon

1 In a large pot (to hold the broccoli later on), cook the rice as per the package instructions.

2 Meanwhile, wash the broccoli and chop it into $1/2$-inch pieces.

3 Five minutes before the rice is done, after about 15 minutes, lift the lid, quickly toss in the broccoli, and cover it back up. Do not stir since the broccoli will essentially steam on top of the rice. Cook for the remaining 5 minutes.

4 Remove the pan from the heat and let it stand, covered, for 5 to 10 minutes. Add the Parmesan, lemon juice, salt, and pepper, and stir to combine.

Health Benefits

One of the reigning kings of superfoods, broccoli is believed to protect against cancer of the colon, prostate, lung, and breast, as well as heart disease. It may also help fight osteoporosis, cataracts, macular degeneration, and birth defects.

Kitchen Tip

Get More Fresh Juice from a Lemon

If you heat a cold lemon either in the microwave or in hot water, you'll get twice as much juice. Rolling and squeezing it helps, too.

When I found this unique spiral fork, it was all I needed to dress up my broccoli rice.

The white plate comes from my own kitchen. Sometimes I shoot extreme close-ups

because the photos make you feel like you can actually smell the food!

Prostate Pasta   MAKES ABOUT 3 CUPS

Attention all men with prostates: Eat tomatoes. They provide lycopene, even more when they're cooked. Studies are showing that lycopene may protect against prostate cancer, so how about a nice pasta marinara? If you think it takes hours to make a good spaghetti sauce, you must try this one. Thirty minutes, tops. And that's mostly waiting time! You'll barely have time to cook your pasta, set the table, and make a salad. You do have a salad with every meal, right? I like this sauce with meatballs, or sometimes I stir in a little cream for a pink sauce. I keep Italian seasoning on hand, which usually contains thyme, oregano, rosemary, marjoram, sage, and basil. If you don't have it, use as many of the listed herbs that you do have to equal $1/2$ teaspoon. I prefer a smoother sauce, so I usually put the canned tomatoes, whether diced or whole, into the food processor and pulse for a few seconds before cooking.

1 tablespoon olive oil

2 cloves garlic, minced

One 28-ounce can diced (or whole) tomatoes in juice

1 tablespoon chopped fresh parsley

$1/2$ teaspoon Italian seasoning

$1/2$ teaspoon sugar

$1/4$ teaspoon salt

Black pepper to taste

2 tablespoons fresh basil, sliced into thin strips

Start-to-Finish
30 minutes

Do I Have What It Takes?
You'll need a large saucepan.

1   In a large saucepan, heat the oil over medium heat. Add the garlic and cook, stirring, for 1 minute, being careful not to let it burn.

2   Add the tomatoes, parsley, Italian seasoning, sugar, salt, and pepper. Bring to a boil, stirring well, then reduce the heat to medium-low and let it gently bubble, uncovered, for 20 minutes.

3   Remove from the heat, stir in the basil, and serve over your favorite pasta.

Health Benefits

It's all about the tomatoes. These antioxidant stars are believed to safeguard you from prostate and other cancers, heart disease, memory loss, and macular degeneration and may even prevent some wrinkles caused by the sun. They might even relieve menopause symptoms.

Shopping List

olive oil ▪ garlic ▪ canned diced tomatoes in juice ▪ fresh parsley ▪ Italian seasoning ▪ sugar ▪ fresh basil

Can you tell it was a beautiful sunny California day when I shot this photo? Even the vintage green glass salt and pepper shakers I found at an antique shop were sparkling. The other "styling" here consists of a kitchen towel, napkin, and my old blue pasta bowl.

Greek Rice

MAKES 6 TO 8 SERVINGS

My stepfamily is Greek and these people know how to eat! If it doesn't have either olive oil, lemon, oregano, or dill, it's not Greek. The rice will cook faster if you heat the stock or water before adding it. If you want the whole Hellenic experience, serve this rice dish with roasted lamb. To do the lamb real Greek style here are the steps: 1. Get a shovel. 2. Dig a big hole in the backyard. 3. Start a wood fire in the hole. 4. Put charcoal briquettes on the wood. 5. Put a whole lamb on a stick over the fire. 6. Turn the lamb until it's done.

1 tablespoon olive oil

$^1/_2$ cup diced green onions (scallions), white and green parts

1 clove garlic, minced

1 cup long-grain rice

2 cups hot chicken or vegetable stock, or water

6 ounces baby spinach, any thick stems removed

1 tablespoon chopped fresh dill

$^1/_2$ teaspoon salt

Black pepper to taste

Start-to-Finish
30 minutes plus 10 minutes to let stand

Do I Have What It Takes?
No special equipment is needed.

Shopping List
olive oil ▪ green onions (scallions) ▪ garlic ▪ rice ▪ chicken or vegetable stock (optional) ▪ baby spinach ▪ fresh dill

1 In a large saucepan, heat the oil over medium heat. Add the onions and garlic and cook, stirring, for 1 minute. Add the rice and cook, stirring, for 1 minute.

2 Add the hot stock or water, bring to a boil, then stir in the spinach, dill, salt, and pepper. Cover, reduce the heat, and simmer for 15 minutes. Remove from the heat and let stand, covered, for 10 minutes before serving.

Health Benefits

Luckily for the Greeks, spinach is a true superfood. It's believed to protect against cancer, heart disease, hypertension and stroke, osteoporosis, cataracts, and macular degeneration. And that's not all. It may also improve your skin and even slow down aging of the brain.

I searched everywhere for something with a Greek motif, and this blue plate was it. Okay, it's not exactly Greek, but if you drink three shots of ouzo and squint your eyes, this is a Greek plate. I chose a two-tone table using the traditional colors of blue and white, which I created with two napkins.

Tabouli MAKES 3 CUPS

Middle Eastern food is some of the best around. Tabouli sounds exotic but it's pretty easy to make. Every single ingredient in this Arabic dish is bursting with healthy goodness. Although traditional tabouli, also spelled tabbouleh, contains mint, I never thought it was worth buying the whole bunch just for 2 tablespoons, and besides, the other flavors are so dominant I don't miss the mint. You can certainly add 1 or 2 tablespoons of fresh chopped mint if you choose. Be sure to use a fine- or medium-grain bulgur that can be soaked and does not require cooking. While the bulgur soaks, you can prepare the rest of the ingredients. Italian parsley has more flavor than the curly kind, but you can use either one. The tomato is added just before serving because tomatoes that have been refrigerated never taste as good so if you make this in advance, don't dice and add the tomatoes until you're ready to serve. Tabouli is traditionally served with romaine lettuce leaves to use as scoopers.

$^1/_2$ cup uncooked bulgur wheat

1 cup boiling water

1 cup chopped fresh Italian parsley

$^1/_3$ cup green onions (scallions), use white and green parts

3 tablespoons fresh lemon juice

1 tablespoon olive oil

$^1/_4$ teaspoon salt

Black pepper to taste

1 medium tomato, finely diced and drained or patted dry

1 In a medium bowl, place the bulgur and add the boiling water. Cover with a plate and let stand for about 30 minutes or until the bulgur is tender and the water is mostly absorbed.

2 Place the softened bulgur in a sieve and drain well, pressing out as much water as you can (or you can drain it just by squeezing with your hands).

3 In a medium bowl, place the drained bulgur. Add the parsley, green onions, lemon juice, olive oil, salt, and pepper. Stir well, cover, and refrigerate until ready to serve. Before serving, stir in the diced tomato.

Kitchen Tip
Don't Refrigerate Tomatoes

If you do, they won't taste as good.

Health Benefits

Bulgur contains lots of fiber, which can help prevent constipation and hemorrhoids. Whole grains also help to stabilize blood sugar and may help protect against high blood pressure, heart disease, and cancer. Besides eliminating bad breath, parsley is a gold mine of antioxidants that may help prevent heart disease, high blood pressure, osteoporosis, and cancer. It's also a digestive aid and is recommended for a healthy urinary tract. Onions are good detoxifiers and are also reported to reduce the risk of blood clots, heart disease, high blood pressure, and memory loss.

Start-to-Finish
35 minutes

Do I Have What It Takes?
A sieve is helpful but not necessary.

Shopping List
bulgur wheat ▪ parsley ▪ green onions (scallions) ▪ lemon ▪ olive oil ▪ tomato

This vibrant mosaic platter was the only one in the store and it had a huge crack through the middle and was missing a bead on the rim as well. I still wanted it, so I offered to pay half price for it and here it is. The crack is under the blue plate and the serving spoon covers the missing bead. The napkin ring is actually two of my bracelets.

Vegetable Sides

Broccoli with a Bite   MAKES 2 TO 4 SERVINGS

Lemon is such a great addition to broccoli, and broccoli is such a great addition to your health regime. You'll need 1 large crown of broccoli to get 4 cups of florets, and if you don't have a steamer basket you can cook the broccoli in $^1/_2$ inch of water, which is essentially the same as steaming. The garlic should be sliced lengthwise to expose as much of it as possible, but watch the heat carefully because garlic can burn quickly. For company, or if you're taking pictures for a cookbook, you can garnish the final dish with strips of lemon zest.

4 cups broccoli florets

1 tablespoon olive oil

2 cloves garlic, sliced in half lengthwise

2 tablespoons fresh lemon juice

$^1/_8$ teaspoon salt

Black pepper to taste

Strips of lemon zest (optional), for garnish

Start-to-Finish
10 minutes

Do I Have What It Takes?
A steamer basket is helpful but not required.

Shopping List
broccoli ▪ olive oil ▪ garlic ▪ lemon

1 In a medium saucepan, steam the broccoli in a wire basket for 5 minutes or until the florets are as crisp or tender as you like. Remove the broccoli to a serving bowl, cover to keep warm, and set aside.

2 While the broccoli steams, in another medium saucepan, heat the oil over medium heat. Add the garlic pieces, cut side down, and cook until both sides are brown but not burned, about 3 minutes, turning the garlic over once. Discard the garlic, leaving the flavored oil in the pan.

3 Remove the saucepan from heat and let cool for about 2 minutes. Stir in the lemon juice, salt, and pepper. Pour over the steamed broccoli and stir until well combined. Garnish with strips of lemon zest (optional).

Health Benefits

Broccoli has been widely reported to reduce the risk of cancer and heart disease. It may also boost your immune system and protect you from cataracts and osteoporosis.

This discount store plate is actually sitting on the edge of a metal picture frame

I had hanging on the wall. I tried to hide the picture of a peach-colored flower (that I took)

under the plate of broccoli but you can still see part of it on the right side.

Seven-Minute Creamy Carrots

MAKES 4 TO 6 SERVINGS

So easy, so healthy, so quick. You can either peel or scrub the carrots and don't be tempted to use more water in the beginning. You are really steaming the carrots and want to retain all the water since it contains some of the nutrients. I use 4 or 5 large carrots for this recipe. Some carrots are sweeter than others, so the pinch of sugar is optional.

4 cups sliced carrots ($1/4$ inch thick)

$1/3$ cup water

$1/4$ cup milk

2 teaspoons cornstarch

Dash of salt and black pepper

Pinch of sugar (optional)

Start-to-Finish
20 minutes

Do I Have What It Takes?
No special equipment is needed.

Shopping List
carrots ▪ milk ▪ cornstarch ▪ sugar (optional)

1   In a small saucepan, place the carrots with the water and bring to a boil. Cover, reduce the heat to medium-low, and cook for 5 minutes, stirring once or twice.

2   In a small bowl or in the measuring cup, whisk together the milk and cornstarch and add to the carrots. Cook, uncovered and stirring, until thick and creamy, 2 to 3 minutes. Season to taste.

Health Benefits

Carrots, especially cooked ones, may support your immune system, eyesight, and memory, and might also defend against lung and other cancers as well as heart disease.

Is this close enough for ya? This was the very first picture I took for this book

and it was right after I got my new macro lens. It was the photo that motivated me to

photograph the entire book myself.

Spinach with Sweet Walnuts

MAKES 4 SERVINGS

Spinach is one of the reigning royalty of superfoods and it turns out that cooked spinach provides even more health benefits than raw. It used to be time consuming to wash spinach but with the prewashed bags of beautiful baby spinach available everywhere, this dish takes very little work.

1 tablespoon sugar

1 tablespoon water

$1/4$ cup walnut pieces

1 teaspoon olive oil

1 clove garlic, minced

One 9-ounce bag baby spinach

$1/4$ teaspoon salt

Black pepper to taste

Start-to-Finish
20 minutes

Do I Have What It Takes?
No special equipment is needed.

Shopping List
sugar ▪ walnuts ▪ olive oil ▪ garlic ▪ spinach

1 In a small saucepan, dissolve the sugar in the water over medium heat. Add the walnuts and cook, stirring, until the liquid is gone, about 5 minutes. Remove the nuts to a large plate and separate them so they don't stick.

2 In a large fry pan, heat the oil over medium heat. Add the garlic and cook, stirring, for 1 minute, being careful not to let it burn. Add the spinach and cook, stirring occasionally, until it's wilted, about 5 minutes. Stir in the walnuts, salt, and pepper.

Health Benefits

Here's why we should all eat spinach: It's reported to protect against cancer, hypertension and stroke, heart disease, osteoporosis, and aging of the brain. It may also fend off birth defects, macular degeneration, and cataracts. Evidence suggests that walnuts can reduce the risk of coronary artery disease and diabetes. Walnuts may also boost your immune system and lower your cholesterol, triglycerides, and blood pressure.

I cheated a bit on this picture. For my plate, I used a cake stand that I found at a T.J. Maxx in Chicago. If you look through the glass you can see a bit of the pedestal base. Since I was alone, I had to hold the fork with my right hand and shoot with my left. It only took about fifty tries to get it straight and in focus.

Kale with Sweet Onions

MAKES 4 TO 6 SERVINGS

I have to admit that kale is not my favorite green, but that wasn't going to stop me from eating it once I heard how important this cruciferous vegetable was to my health, especially my bones. Then I remembered that song, "A spoonful of sugar helps the medicine go down. . ." To me, kale is the medicine that will keep me healthy, and now I have a delicious way to enjoy it. If you're lucky enough to find sweet Vidalia or Maui onions, they are perfect for this recipe, but any onion will do, from Spanish to Bermuda, red, white, or brown.

1 bunch kale

2 teaspoons olive oil

2 cups coarsely chopped onion

2 teaspoons red wine vinegar

2 teaspoons balsamic vinegar

2 teaspoons sugar

$1/4$ teaspoon salt

Black pepper to taste

Start-to-Finish
25 minutes

Do I Have What It Takes?
No special equipment is needed.

Shopping List
kale ▪ olive oil ▪ onions ▪ red wine vinegar ▪ balsamic vinegar ▪ sugar

1   Cut away the center ribs from the kale. Coarsely chop and wash the greens.

2   In a large pot, bring $1/2$ cup water to a boil and add the kale. Cover and cook over medium-low heat until the kale is wilted and soft, about 5 minutes. Remove from the heat.

3   In a large sauté pan, heat the olive oil over medium heat. Add the onions and cook, stirring, until translucent, about 3 minutes. Add the red wine vinegar, balsamic vinegar, sugar, salt, and pepper and cook, stirring regularly, until the onions are nicely browned, about 5 minutes.

4   Stir the cooked and drained kale into the onion mixture and serve.

Health Benefits

Kale may help protect against cancer, osteoporosis, vision loss, high cholesterol, and birth defects. The onions count, too. They may also protect against cancer, heart disease, memory loss, high blood pressure, and blood clots. Onions are also believed to help fight infection.

You can almost see the vintage serving spoon in the background here. This

colorful striped place mat came from Bed Bath & Beyond and cost $2.99.

I'd love to say I planned that pretty reflection of the stripes in the front of the bowl,

but I didn't notice it until I was done.

Mashed Root Vegetables

MAKES 4 TO 6 SERVINGS

This is just delicious—creamy and sweet and so easy to make. Just be sure the vegetables are thoroughly cooked and soft. You can also add a handful of cauliflower or broccoli to the steamer for even extra antioxidant punch. If you don't have chicken or vegetable stock on hand, be sure to save some of the cooking water to add to the puree.

I sweet potato

I turnip

I carrot

I parsnip

I rutabaga

I potato

$1/3$ cup vegetable or chicken stock, or reserved cooking liquid

$1/2$ teaspoon salt

Black pepper to taste

Start-to-Finish
30 minutes

Do I Have What It Takes?
You'll need a food processor, and a steamer basket is helpful but a large pot with a lid will do.

Shopping List
sweet potato ▪ turnip ▪ carrot ▪ parsnip ▪ rutabaga ▪ potato ▪ vegetable or chicken stock (optional)

1   Peel and chop the vegetables into 1-inch chunks. Using a steamer basket (you can also "steam" them in about an inch of water) in a large covered pot, steam the vegetables for 15 to 20 minutes. Pierce a harder vegetable, like the rutabaga or carrot, with a thin knife to test for doneness.

2   In a food processor fitted with a metal blade, place the slightly cooled vegetables along with the stock or reserved cooking liquid, salt, and pepper. Process until smooth and creamy, adjusting the consistency with more liquid if needed.

Health Benefits

There are almost too many to name, but here it goes: Possible protection against cancer, heart disease, high blood pressure, osteoporosis, stroke, memory loss, constipation, and hypertension. This winning combination of veggies may also boost your immune system, lower your cholesterol, and protect your eyesight and lungs.

Are these mashed vegetables beautiful or what? They were so pretty,

I thought they deserved to be in an equally pretty antique glass dish that I found

at a strip of antique shops in Pomona, California. I got the spoon there, too.

Roasted Vegetables

MAKES 4 TO 6 SERVINGS

How much do I love this dish? It's a treat for the eyes and stomach and goes well with anything—roast chicken, meat loaf, broiled fish, barbecued steaks, leg of lamb, you name it. Plus, you can add even more of your favorite vegetables like green beans, zucchini, or those cute little yellow squashes.

$^1/_2$ pound small red skinned potatoes

I medium sweet potato

2 medium carrots

I yellow bell pepper

I fennel bulb

I red onion

I garlic bulb

$^1/_4$ cup olive oil

Salt and black pepper to taste

Start-to-Finish
45 minutes, mostly unattended

Do I Have What It Takes?
You'll need a large baking sheet.

1 Preheat the oven to 450°F. Lightly grease a large baking sheet with olive oil.

2 Prepare the vegetables as follows:

- Red skinned potatoes: wash and scrub clean, do not peel, cut into quarters

- Sweet potato and carrots: peel and cut into large bite-size pieces

- Yellow bell pepper: cut and core, removing seeds and membrane, cut into large strips

- Fennel: use bulb only, remove tough outer layers, cut into bite-size chunks or slices

- Onion: peel, chop into large sections

- Garlic: leave bulb whole but slice in half crosswise across the middle

3 On the baking sheet, place the prepared vegetables and toss with the olive oil, salt, and pepper. Roast for about 30 minutes, shaking or stirring once.

Health Benefits

These many beautiful colors provide a bevy of health-promoting benefits. There are strong indications that these vegetables may provide protection against cancer, heart disease, and stroke. They may also safeguard against bone loss, memory loss, arthritis, and asthma. Your lungs and eye health may be protected, cholesterol lowered, and circulation improved. If you eat the garlic it may also be beneficial for those with bronchitis.

I couldn't find the right plate for my vegetables so I took this one off the wall.

It was hanging up for decoration and I don't think it was meant for food but it

sure looks good. I set it on my den coffee table that's made out of

an old loading dock cart.

I Can't Believe It's Cauliflower

MAKES 6 TO 8 SERVINGS

You can whip this up in no time, and you'll have two super-duper superfoods in one. It's whipped cauliflower with sweet potato, and what a great way for those of us who don't love cauliflower to add this important cruciferous vegetable to our diet, as well as some high-antioxidant sweet potato. Friends will swear you put sugar in this mashed mountain of goodness. Try to cut the vegetables into similarly-sized chunks for even steaming. One of those folding steamer baskets is ideal. You'll need half a head of cauliflower and one medium sweet potato. I used milk, but you can also use chicken or vegetable stock, or even water, for the liquid.

2 cups chopped cauliflower (1-inch chunks)

2 cups peeled, chopped sweet potato (1-inch chunks)

$^1/_2$ cup 1% low-fat milk, warmed

$^1/_2$ tablespoon unsalted butter

$^1/_4$ teaspoon salt

Black pepper to taste

Start-to-Finish
25 minutes

Do I Have What It Takes?
You'll need a food processor, and a steamer basket is helpful but not essential.

Shopping List
cauliflower ▪ sweet potato
▪ milk ▪ unsalted butter

1   Steam the cauliflower and sweet potato in a steamer basket until soft, 7 to 10 minutes. If you don't have a steamer basket, you can cook them in a covered pot in about 1 inch of water and then drain.

2   In a food processor fitted with the metal blade, place the steamed vegetables along with the milk, butter, salt, and pepper. Whip and serve.

Health Benefits

Both of these vegetable superstars are reported to protect against cancer and heart disease. Sweet potatoes also have a reputation for boosting your immune system, reducing blood pressure, and protecting your lungs, eyesight, and bones. Cauliflower is also believed to lower cholesterol levels, help fight stress, and reduce the risk of stroke.

Cookies that Count

Chocolate-Almond Biscotti MAKES 24 BISCOTTI

I was surprised how easy it was the first time I made biscotti. People say, "I can't believe you make biscotti," assuming it's a complicated task, but when your goal is to bake something dry, how can you go wrong? These keep well, and they make fabulous gifts if you can part with them. If I'm pressured enough I will throw in 2 tablespoons of mini chocolate chips. Have you ever tried biscotti dunked in warm milk? M-m-m-m.

²/₃ cup whole raw almonds

1³/₄ cups all-purpose flour

¹/₃ cup unsweetened cocoa

1 teaspoon baking soda

¹/₄ teaspoon salt

3 large eggs

1 cup sugar

1 teaspoon vanilla extract

Start-to-Finish
2 hours

Do I Have What It Takes?
You'll need a large baking sheet and parchment paper. A wide scraper and a long serrated knife are helpful but not essential.

1 Preheat the oven to 350°F. Line a large baking sheet with parchment paper.

2 Spread the almonds on another ungreased baking sheet and toast them in the oven for 7 to 10 minutes, until they look golden and, well. . . toasted. Spread the almonds on a dinner plate to cool. Reduce the oven temperature to 300°F.

3 Into a medium bowl, sift together the flour, cocoa, baking soda, and salt.

4 In a large mixing bowl, beat the eggs using an electric mixer on medium speed. Take 1 minute to slowly add the sugar while beating. Continue beating until nice and thick, 5 minutes. Stir in the vanilla.

5 Coarsely chop the cooled almonds. With the mixer on low speed, add the flour mixture to the egg mixture. Stir in the chopped almonds.

6 Remove the mixture to a floured work surface and knead 10 times. The mixture will be sticky, but you can use a scraper to lift it.

7 Transfer the mixture to the lined baking sheet and shape into a log about 14 x 5 inches. Bake for 45 minutes.

8 Remove from the oven and cool, undisturbed on the baking sheet, for 10 minutes. Transfer the log from your baking sheet onto a cutting board and slice into $^1/_2$-inch-thick pieces. A serrated knife works well here.

9 Carefully place the slices directly on the oven rack and bake for 10 to 15 minutes more, or until dry. Remove the biscotti from the oven with a metal spatula and cool completely on a wire rack.

Health Benefits

Cocoa may protect your arteries, immune system, and heart. Yippee! Almonds help keep your cholesterol in check, protect your heart, and may help reduce the risk of diabetes and Alzheimer's.

Shopping List
whole raw almonds ▪ flour ▪ unsweetened cocoa ▪ baking soda ▪ eggs ▪ sugar ▪ vanilla extract

You'd never know it but that's not a real paper bag, it's a ceramic vase made to look like a bag. It's hard as a rock, and it's so unusual. I bought it in Chicago at a home decorating store.

Cholesterol Buster Cookies

MAKES 24 COOKIES

This delicious oatmeal-prune cookie is my absolute favorite. Chopping the prunes (dried plums, to be politically correct) is much easier in a food processor, but make sure you get the pitted ones! The batter can be made ahead and refrigerated or baked right away. If you don't have parchment paper, just lightly grease the cookie sheet with butter. To tout the many health benefits of this cookie, I simply say, "Have an oatmeal-prune, it'll keep you immune."

I cup whole-grain pastry flour

$^1/_2$ teaspoon baking soda

$^1/_8$ teaspoon cinnamon

$^1/_8$ teaspoon salt

$1^1/_4$ cups regular oats, not instant

$^1/_4$ cup oat bran

2 tablespoons ground flaxseed meal

3 tablespoons unsalted butter, softened

5 tablespoons canola oil

$^1/_3$ cup white sugar

$^1/_3$ cup light brown sugar

I large egg

$^1/_2$ teaspoon vanilla extract

$^1/_2$ cup diced pitted prunes (about 12 big ones)

Start-to-Finish
40 minutes

Do I Have What It Takes?
You'll need a large baking sheet.

1   Preheat the oven to 350°F. Line a large baking sheet with parchment paper.

2   Into a large bowl, sift the flour, baking soda, cinnamon, and salt. Stir in the oats, oat bran, and flaxseed meal.

3   In another bowl with an electric mixer on medium-high speed, beat the butter and oil until blended. Slowly add the white and brown sugars and egg, beating until thick, for 2 to 3 minutes. Stir in the vanilla.

4   With the mixer on low speed, add the flour mixture to the egg mixture, then add the prunes. Do not overmix.

5   Shape the dough into $1^1/_2$-inch balls and place at least 2 inches apart on the baking sheet. Press them flat with your hand or the bottom of a glass. Bake for 13 to 15 minutes. Remove immediately to a wire rack to cool.

Kitchen Tip

Always Store Ground Flaxseed Meal in Your Freezer

Once the flax is ground, it is very susceptible to turning rancid. I use it often in baking and always keep it in my freezer.

Health Benefits

Oats are known to lower cholesterol, help control weight, and keep blood sugar stabilized. Flax and walnuts provide omega-3s to protect your heart. Prunes may strengthen the immune system and urinary tract, protect against memory loss, and slow down aging. The combined high fiber in this cookie may protect against constipation, diverticulitis, high blood pressure, heart disease, and colon cancer.

Shopping List
whole-grain pastry flour ▪ baking soda ▪ cinnamon ▪ oats ▪ oat bran ▪ ground flaxseed meal ▪ unsalted butter ▪ canola oil ▪ white sugar ▪ brown sugar ▪ egg ▪ vanilla extract ▪ pitted prunes

The cookie picture had to reflect the fun that is cookies. So I looked around the house until I saw the miniature tea book and then found one of my favorite teddy bears. I gave him the book and placed him in the saucer that goes with the teacup. Pictured is a Cholesterol Buster and a Peanut Butter cookie.

Peanut Butter Cookies

MAKES ABOUT 30 COOKIES

These are not low-fat but most of it is heart-healthy fat. I recommend using an all-natural peanut butter, like Laura Scudder (ingredients: peanuts, salt). I prefer the chunky style, but use smooth if you like. If your health food store sells peanut butter that includes the brown skins on the peanut, you'll get even more healthful polyphenols. Using a melon baller to shape the cookies makes it go faster and your cookies will all be the same size. Adding extra peanuts really enhances the peanut-y flavor and you can chop them nice and fine in a food processor. If I'm asked nicely, I will sometimes throw in a handful of mini chocolate chips.

1 1/4 cups all-purpose flour

1/2 teaspoon baking powder

1/2 teaspoon baking soda

1/4 teaspoon salt

1/4 cup ground flaxseed meal

3 tablespoons unsalted butter, softened

3 tablespoons canola oil

1/2 cup peanut butter (I use chunky)

1/2 cup white sugar

1/3 cup light brown sugar

1 large egg

1/2 teaspoon vanilla extract

1/2 cup finely diced dry roasted lightly salted peanuts (optional)

Start-to-Finish
40 minutes

Do I Have What It Takes?
You'll need a large baking sheet.

1 Preheat the oven to 350°F. Line a large baking sheet with parchment paper or lightly grease with butter.

2 Into a bowl or onto waxed paper, sift together the flour, baking powder, baking soda, and salt. Stir in the flaxseed meal.

3 In a large bowl using an electric mixer at medium speed, beat the butter, oil, and peanut butter until well combined, about a minute. Continue beating and slowly add the white and brown sugars, then the egg and vanilla. Combine well.

4 With the mixer on the lowest speed, add the flour mixture, then the peanuts, if using. Do not overmix.

5 Shape into 1 1/2-inch balls and place 2 inches apart on the baking sheet. Flatten the cookies by making a criss-cross design with a fork, a wet one if it sticks. Bake for 10 to 12 minutes or until the edges are lightly browned. Remove from the sheet right away to a wire cooling rack.

Health Benefits

Peanuts contain heart-healthy omega-3 fatty acids, which may protect your heart, lower cholesterol and blood pressure, and even improve your hair, nails, and skin. Nuts also provide protein and fiber and may also protect against diabetes, hypertension, eye diseases, and cancer. Flaxseed increases the fiber even more as well as the omega-3s, and may safeguard against heart disease, vision loss, and prostate, colon, and breast cancer.

Lemon Bars

MAKES 9 TO 16 SQUARES

Pucker up. These have some serious lemon flavor so make sure you can handle it. Here's proof that delicious lemon bars don't have to be full of butter. Just a little is all you'll need. Either a box grater or a Microplane zester can be used to obtain the grated lemon zest. If you use a hand-held lemon zester, the resulting long curly strips of peel should be chopped up a little. Be sure to scrub the lemons well before grating the zest and do that before you squeeze them for juice. Also, I find that a stand mixer is too big for this small job, so use your electric hand mixer and a smaller bowl. And don't even think about using bottled juice or dried lemon peel!

CRUST

2¹/₂ tablespoons unsalted butter, softened

2 tablespoons canola oil

¹/₃ cup sugar

1 cup all-purpose flour

TOPPING

3 large eggs

²/₃ cup sugar

¹/₂ cup fresh lemon juice (2 lemons)

¹/₄ cup all-purpose flour

Zest of 2 lemons

Powdered sugar for serving

Start-to-Finish
50 minutes

Do I Have What It Takes?
You'll need an 8-inch square baking pan and a lemon zester or box grater.

1. Preheat the oven to 350°F. Lightly grease an 8-inch square baking pan with butter.

2. To make the crust, in a medium bowl with an electric hand mixer on medium-high speed, beat the butter, oil, and sugar for 1 minute. With the mixer on the lowest speed, add the flour and mix for about 15 seconds until the mixture resembles very coarse crumbs.

3. Transfer the mixture to the baking pan and press down firmly and evenly. Bake for 20 minutes or until golden. Reduce the oven temperature to 300°F when the crust is done.

4. Meanwhile, prepare the topping. In a medium bowl with the electric hand mixer, beat the eggs and sugar on medium speed until thick, about 3 minutes. Beat in the juice, flour, and lemon zest. Don't worry if the batter seems too liquid.

5. Pour the egg mixture over the hot crust. Bake in the 300°F oven for 18 to 20 minutes, or until firm. Cool completely in the pan. Sprinkle with powdered sugar and cut into squares.

Health Benefits

These are much lower in saturated fat than regular lemon squares. Besides that, the lemon peel and juice contain powerful antioxidants that can protect against cancer, heart disease, and stroke. They are also good detoxifiers and can help regulate blood sugar and cholesterol, as well as strengthen your immune system and eyesight.

Shopping List
unsalted butter ▪ canola oil ▪ sugar ▪ flour ▪ eggs ▪ lemons ▪ powdered sugar

Here I go with my macro lens again. For the plate I chose a ceramic tile that was given to me by a former staffer at my talk show. It took about three hours of trial and error to get the shiny edges of the lemon bar as well as the powdered sugar top to both come out at the same time, but I finally got it.

Fudgey Brownies MAKES 12 BROWNIES

I'm not saying you can eat brownies every day but when you've just gotta have them, these are healthier than most. Because I use powdered cocoa instead of solid, these have way less fat, especially less saturated fat. But be aware—not all unsweetened powdered cocoa is the same. Some of the expensive ones are very high in fat so read the labels. I use Ghirardelli and Hershey's brands. Everything gets mixed with a spoon, no electric mixer.

1/4 cup (1/2 stick) unsalted butter

1 1/2 cups all-purpose flour

2/3 cup unsweetened cocoa

1/2 teaspoon baking powder

1/4 teaspoon salt

1/4 cup canola oil

1 1/2 cups sugar

3 large eggs, lightly beaten

1 1/2 teaspoons vanilla extract

1 cup coarsely chopped walnuts, plus an extra 1/2 cup for topping (optional)

Start-to-Finish
45 minutes

Do I Have What It Takes?
You'll need a 9-inch square baking pan.

1   Preheat the oven to 350°F. Lightly grease the bottom only and not the sides of a 9-inch square baking pan.

2   In a small saucepan or in the microwave, melt the butter and place in a large bowl to cool. In another bowl or onto waxed paper, sift together the flour, cocoa, baking powder, and salt. Set aside.

3   To the cooled butter, add the oil and sugar all at once and stir briefly with a large spoon or "spoonula." Add the eggs and vanilla all at once and stir just until combined. The mixture will be thick and grainy but that's okay. Fold in the flour mixture and the 1 cup of walnuts.

4   The mixture will be thick, so pat it into the pan, using your fingers or the back of a wet spoon. Sprinkle with more walnuts, if desired.

5   Bake for 25 minutes. The brownies will still give a little when you touch the top but, don't be tempted to overbake. Let the brownies cool in the pan or at least try to wait that long.

Health Benefits

You'll be glad to know that chocolate may actually lower your risk of heart disease as well as strengthen your immune system. And walnuts, besides providing protein, are one of the best things you can eat for your cholesterol. Evidence strongly suggests they protect the heart and they also may protect against diabetes, high blood pressure, and cancer.

Shopping List
unsalted butter ▪ flour ▪ unsweetened cocoa ▪ baking powder ▪ canola oil ▪ sugar ▪ eggs ▪ vanilla extract ▪ walnuts

I'm one of those people who save wrapping paper and have been known to reuse certain papers more than once. Some date back to the early '70s. This is some of my newer tissue paper, which I chose because brownies make great gifts. And if those look like my teeth marks on the front brownie, I assure you I have much more self-control than that.

Meringues   **MAKES ABOUT 24 COOKIES**

What can I say? They're fat-free, and they taste like cotton candy. A stand mixer makes this super easy to do, especially if you use the wire whisk attachment. If it's raining or humid outside, skip this recipe. The meringues need to dry out. To shape them I use 2 spoons, but you can also use a pastry bag or even a plastic storage bag with the corner cut out. The idea is to bake them until they are totally dry but not browned. They'll keep for weeks in an airtight container at room temperature. Oh, and they're fragile too, but you'll find that out as soon as you squeeze one too hard. I dare you to try to eat just one.

3 large egg whites at room temperature

$^1/_8$ teaspoon cream of tartar

1 cup sugar

$^1/_2$ teaspoon vanilla extract

Variations

- For a soft, marshmallow-type middle, bake at 250°F for 45 minutes, then remove to cool on a wire cooling rack.

- For a chocolate swirl, melt 3 tablespoons semi-sweet chocolate chips in a microwave, let cool, and lightly swirl into the batter using a toothpick.

- For a simpler chocolate fix, toss about $^1/_4$ cup mini chocolate chips into the batter just before mounding.

1   Set the oven racks to hold 2 baking sheets and preheat the oven to 200°F. Line 2 large baking sheets with parchment paper.

2   In a large bowl with an electric mixer on medium speed, beat the egg whites until foamy, about 2 minutes. Add the cream of tartar and beat until fairly stiff, about 3 minutes.

3   Slowly add the sugar, 1 tablespoon at a time, then beat until very stiff and glossy, about 5 minutes. Add the vanilla and beat for another minute.

4   Using 2 spoons, drop 2-inch mounds of the batter onto the baking sheets. Bake for 1 hour, rotating the sheets halfway through for even baking. Turn off the oven and leave cookies inside the closed oven for another hour.

Kitchen Tip

Don't Refrigerate Chocolate

It has a negative effect on the texture.

Health Benefits

Let's be honest here. Except for being fat-free, the benefits of meringues are strictly psychological. But if the daily stresses of life make you reach for something sweet, and that something is like a taste of sweet billowy clouds straight from heaven, and suddenly your stresses are floating away, and since we all know stress can weaken your immune system, then would I be wrong in saying that meringues are beneficial to the immune system? You see my point.

Start-to-Finish
2 hours and 30 minutes

Do I Have What It Takes?
You'll need an electric mixer, 2 large baking sheets, and parchment paper.

Shopping List
eggs ▪ cream of tartar ▪ sugar ▪ vanilla extract

Since meringues taste like fluffy clouds, I wanted to put them on clouds so I used colored netting. Although I included the chocolate swirl and chocolate chip, I still like the plain meringues best. In setting up this picture I squeezed a few meringues too hard and they broke. I ate them. All five.

Fig Bars

MAKES 12 TO 16 SQUARES

Here's a delicious way to get lots of fiber in a chewy, satisfying bar. It's sweet enough for dessert, but not too sweet to pinch-hit as an emergency snack bar. Any kind of figs will do, but be sure you cut the hard little stem off the end of each dried fig. After that, a food processor makes the chopping of the figs a breeze. The cooked fig mixture will cool a lot faster if transferred from the pot onto a dinner plate and spread out.

1 1/2 cups dried figs (one 8-ounce bag), finely chopped

3/4 cup water

1/4 cup sugar

1 heaping tablespoon semi-sweet chocolate chips

1/4 cup (1/2 stick) unsalted butter, softened

1/4 cup canola oil

1/2 cup light brown sugar

1 cup all-purpose flour

1/2 teaspoon baking soda

1/4 teaspoon salt

1 cup quick-cooking oats

1/3 cup finely chopped walnuts

Start-to-Finish
1 hour

Do I Have What It Takes?
You'll need a 9-inch square baking pan.

1   In a medium saucepan over medium heat, cook the figs, water, sugar, and chocolate chips, stirring a few times, until thick, about 5 minutes. Spread the mixture onto a dinner plate to cool.

2   Meanwhile, preheat the oven to 350°F. Lightly grease a 9-inch square baking pan.

3   In a mixing bowl with an electric mixer on medium-high speed, beat the butter, oil, and brown sugar for 3 minutes, scraping the sides of the bowl down at least once.

4   In another bowl or onto waxed paper, sift together the flour, baking soda, and salt, then stir in the oats.

5   With the mixer on low speed, add the oat mixture to the butter mixture and mix just until blended.

6   Press 2/3 of the mixture in the bottom of the baking pan. Top with the cooled fig mixture, trying not to let it touch the edges of the pan. Stir the walnuts into the rest of the oat mixture and press it firmly over the fig mixture.

7   Bake for about 30 minutes or until the top is golden. Cool in the pan, then cut into squares.

Health Benefits

Oats are known to lower cholesterol and help stabilize blood sugar. They can also help with diverticulitis, diabetes, constipation, and weight loss. They boost the immune system and can protect your bones and heart. Figs have calcium for strong bones and are high in fiber, which always helps with moving things along. They may also protect against heart disease and colon cancer.

Shopping List
dried figs ▪ sugar ▪ chocolate chips ▪ unsalted butter ▪ canola oil ▪ brown sugar ▪ flour ▪ baking soda ▪ quick oats ▪ walnuts

This picture took a long, long time. . . I'm not kidding. It was almost five hours before I got a shot that I liked. I tried different colored backgrounds, plates, cake stands, lighting from the side, lighting from behind, etc. I finally got one I liked using an embroidered tea towel.

Clear Conscience Cakes

Sweet Potato Chocolate Cake

MAKES ONE 9-INCH CAKE

This is the recipe I've been asked for more than any other. Everyone loves this delicious, moist cake, especially Earl, my makeup artist. He was shocked when I told him it contains sweet potato which, by the way, is just about the highest single vegetable source of beta-carotene. I've tried baking and steaming the sweet potato, but I get the best results with boiling it. You can then mash it with a fork or put it through a ricer. Just make sure it's not lumpy. I usually mash it with a fork and spread it out on a plate to cool quickly. Frosting cakes right in the pan means fewer dishes and easy storage. Plus, it takes less frosting than doing all the sides. Just a note about unsweetened cocoa: they are not all the same so read the labels. Some of the expensive ones are much higher in fat. I use Hershey's or Ghirardelli.

²/₃ cup cooked mashed sweet potato (1 medium sweet potato)

1¹/₄ cups all-purpose flour

¹/₄ cup unsweetened cocoa

1 teaspoon baking powder

1 teaspoon baking soda

¹/₈ teaspoon salt

¹/₂ cup low-fat buttermilk

¹/₂ teaspoon vanilla extract

¹/₂ cup canola oil

¹/₂ cup sugar

2 large eggs

FROSTING

2 tablespoons unsalted butter, softened

2 tablespoons reduced-fat sour cream

1 Preheat the oven to 350°F. Lightly grease a 9-inch round cake pan with butter.

2 Peel and chop the sweet potato into 1-inch chunks. Boil in a pot with just enough water to cover until tender, about 5 minutes. Drain, mash with a fork (or put through a ricer), and let cool.

3 Into a bowl or onto waxed paper, sift together the flour, cocoa, baking powder, baking soda, and salt.

4 In a small bowl, combine the buttermilk, vanilla, and ²/₃ cup of the cooled sweet potato until well blended.

5 In a large mixing bowl with an electric mixer on medium-high speed, beat the oil while slowly adding the sugar. Add the eggs, 1 at a time, and continue beating for 5 minutes.

6 With the mixer on the lowest speed, add the sweet potato mixture followed by the flour mixture.

7 Pour the batter into the cake pan. Bake for 25 minutes or until a toothpick inserted in the center comes out clean. Cool completely in the pan on a wire cooling rack.

8 Meanwhile, prepare the frosting. In a medium bowl with an electric hand mixer, beat the butter and sour cream. Mix in the confectioners' sugar, cocoa, and vanilla. Beat until smooth, 3 to 4 minutes. Adjust the consistency, if necessary, by adding a little milk or sour cream.

9 Cover the top of the cooled cake with the frosting.

Health Benefits

The sweet potato is an antiaging champion. It has tons of beta-carotene, which may protect your lungs and eyesight, strengthen your immune system, and protect against heart disease and cancer. Cocoa is now reported to contain antioxidants and may actually boost your immune system and protect your heart, too!

The blue fabric under this beautiful square blue plate was the dramatic look I wanted for my very special cake. I think we all know what happened to that forkful the minute I got my shot.

1 1/2 cups confectioners' sugar

1 1/2 tablespoons unsweetened cocoa

1/4 teaspoon vanilla extract

1 tablespoon milk or sour cream to soften

Start-to-Finish
1 hour plus cooling and frosting time, less if you cook and cool the sweet potato in advance

Do I Have What It Takes?
You'll need a 9-inch round baking pan, and a potato ricer is helpful but not necessary.

Shopping List
sweet potato ▪ flour ▪ unsweetened cocoa ▪ baking powder ▪ baking soda ▪ buttermilk ▪ vanilla extract ▪ canola oil ▪ sugar ▪ eggs ▪ unsalted butter ▪ reduced-fat sour cream ▪ confectioners' sugar ▪ milk (optional)

Carrot Cake

If you're Jonesin' for some cake, then pick one that has some nutritional value. Homemade carrot cake is a real treat. This one is moist and delicious and makes a fabulous birthday cake. As with most of the cakes I bake, you cool and frost in the same pan. Shredding carrots is about as much fun as waxing your legs, but you won't regret the hard work. The best results come from a box-style grater. Crushed pineapple in its own juice has the least amount of added sugar, and the best way to thoroughly drain it is to squeeze it in your hand and then squeeze it again in a paper towel.

1 1/2 cups all-purpose flour

1 teaspoon baking powder

1 teaspoon baking soda

3/4 teaspoon cinnamon

1/8 teaspoon nutmeg

1/8 teaspoon allspice

1/4 teaspoon salt

1/3 cup low-fat buttermilk

1 teaspoon vanilla extract

1/4 cup canola oil

1/2 cup sugar

2 large eggs

3/4 cup lightly packed grated carrot (1 great big carrot)

1/2 of an 8-ounce can crushed pineapple in its own juice, well drained

1/2 cup diced walnuts

CREAM CHEESE FROSTING

1 ounce regular cream cheese

1/2 tablespoon unsalted butter, softened

1. Preheat the oven to 350°F. Lightly grease an 8-inch round baking pan with butter.

2. Into a bowl or onto waxed paper, sift together the flour, baking powder, baking soda, cinnamon, nutmeg, allspice, and salt.

3. In a bowl or measuring cup, combine the buttermilk and vanilla.

4. In another bowl with an electric mixer on medium-high speed, beat the oil while slowly adding the sugar. Add the eggs 1 at a time and continue beating until thick, 3 minutes. With mixer on the lowest speed, alternate adding the flour mixture and buttermilk mixture, starting and ending with the flour. Stir in the grated carrots, pineapple, and walnuts, stirring just until combined.

5. Pour the batter into the pan. Bake for 35 minutes or until a toothpick inserted in the center comes out clean. Cool in the pan.

6. Meanwhile, prepare the frosting. In a bowl, beat together the cream cheese, butter, confectioners' sugar, and vanilla and add just enough milk, a little bit at a time, to get a good spreading

consistency. Add orange zest (optional).Spread the frosting on the top of the cooled cake and keep it refrigerated.

Health Benefits

The beta-carotene in carrots can protect against cancer, heart disease, and memory loss and supports your lungs, eyesight, and immune system. Walnuts can also protect your eyes, lower your cholesterol, triglycerides, and blood pressure, strengthen your immune system, and help reduce the risk of diabetes and cancer.

1 cup confectioners' sugar

1/4 teaspoon vanilla extract

Up to 1 tablespoon milk

Zest of 1 orange (optional)

Start-to-Finish
1 hour plus cooling and frosting time

Do I Have What It Takes?
You'll need a 9-inch round baking pan and a box grater.

Shopping List
flour ▪ baking powder ▪ baking soda ▪ cinnamon ▪ nutmeg ▪ allspice ▪ buttermilk ▪ vanilla extract ▪ canola oil ▪ sugar ▪ eggs ▪ carrot ▪ canned crushed pineapple in its own juice ▪ walnuts ▪ cream cheese ▪ unsalted butter ▪ confectioners' sugar ▪ milk ▪ orange (optional)

Well this was not easy. Imagine me holding the cake holder with my left hand and shooting on automatic pilot with my right. It's a wonder I got anything at all. The dots in the background came from the box grater I used to shred the carrots.

Lemon-Blueberry Bundt Cake

Do you love, I mean really love, lemon? This intense, very lemony cake is moist, not too sweet, and just right with tea. Be sure to scrub your lemons well before zesting, which you can do with a box grater, a hand-held lemon zester, or a Microplane. Make sure to take just the yellow zest and leave all the white part behind, and definitely zest the lemons before juicing them. Once the cake is baked, if you don't want to glaze it you can just sift a little powdered sugar on top. And don't even think about using bottled lemon juice!

3 cups all-purpose flour

2 teaspoons baking powder

1 teaspoon baking soda

$1/4$ teaspoon salt

1 cup low-fat buttermilk

$1/4$ cup fresh lemon juice (1 lemon)

1 teaspoon vanilla extract

$1/3$ cup unsalted butter, softened

$1/4$ cup canola oil

$1^1/3$ cups sugar

3 large eggs

Zest of 3 lemons

1 heaping cup blueberries, washed and patted dry

GLAZE

1 cup powdered sugar

1 tablespoon fresh lemon juice

1   Preheat the oven to 350°F. Grease a 10-inch Bundt pan with butter and shake about 2 tablespoons of sugar around the inside to facilitate removal of the cake. Tap out any excess sugar.

2   Into a bowl or onto a sheet of waxed paper, sift together the flour, baking powder, baking soda, and salt.

3   In a small bowl or a measuring cup, combine the buttermilk, lemon juice, and vanilla.

4   In a large bowl using an electric mixer on medium speed, beat the butter and oil for 1 minute. Slowly add the sugar and then the eggs, 1 at a time, and continue beating for 5 minutes. Stir in the lemon zest. With the mixer on the lowest speed, alternate adding the flour mixture and the buttermilk mixture, starting and ending with the flour mixture.

5   Using a large spatula or "spoonula," gently fold in the blueberries. Spoon the batter into the Bundt pan.

6   Bake for about 1 hour. Cool in the pan for 10 minutes, then invert onto a wire rack. It should slip right out. Cool for 15 minutes.

7   Meanwhile, prepare the glaze. Combine the powdered sugar and just enough lemon juice (up to 1 tablespoon) for a nice spreading consistency. Drizzle the top of the cooled cake with the glaze.

Health Benefits

Blueberries are it. They are nutritional superstars that may protect your heart, eyes, skin, urinary tract, and memory. Wait, there's more. They are antiaging, bone-protecting, immune-boosting brain food, and possible defenders against Alzheimer's, diabetes, senility, and cancer. Lemon juice and the zest are good detoxifiers and might also protect against stroke and cancer.

Start-to-Finish
1 hour and 45 minutes

Do I Have What It Takes?
You'll need a 9- or 10-inch Bundt pan and a box grater or other lemon zester.

Shopping List
flour ▪ baking powder ▪ baking soda ▪ buttermilk ▪ lemons ▪ vanilla extract ▪ unsalted butter ▪ canola oil ▪ sugar ▪ eggs ▪ fresh blueberries ▪ powdered sugar

The glass plate cost about $3.00, and the embroidered tablecloth under it cost a lot more. The teacup was a present, and the antique cake server that you can almost see came from an antique mall in Santa Monica. I shot this in the morning sun, which was nice but warm, so it melted my glaze a bit.

Greek Walnut Cake

My stepmother, Roula, is Greek, and I've grown to love Greek food. Walnut cake, known as *karithopita*, is delicious, but my version has less fat and sugar and more walnuts than most. For the best use of time, prepare the cake first, and cook the syrup while it's baking. Be sure to scrub the orange well before zesting, which you can do with a box grater, hand-held lemon zester, or a Microplane zester. Traditionally this cake is cut into diamond shapes, but you can do your own thing.

1 1/2 cups all-purpose flour

1 1/2 teaspoons baking powder

1/2 teaspoon baking soda

1/2 teaspoon cinnamon

1/4 teaspoon salt

1/3 cup canola oil

1/2 cup sugar

2 large eggs

Grated zest of 1 medium orange

1/2 cup 1% low-fat milk

1 heaping cup finely chopped walnuts

SYRUP

1 cup water

1/2 cup sugar

1 cinnamon stick

2 x 1-inch piece of lemon rind

4 whole cloves

1 Preheat the oven to 350°F. Lightly grease a 9-inch square baking pan with butter.

2 Into a bowl or onto waxed paper, sift together the flour, baking powder, baking soda, cinnamon, and salt.

3 In a large mixing bowl with an electric mixer on medium-high speed, beat the oil while slowly adding the sugar. Add the eggs, 1 at a time, and continue beating for 3 minutes, scraping down the sides of the bowl once. Stir in the orange zest.

4 With the mixer on the lowest speed, alternate adding the flour mixture with the milk, starting and ending with the flour. Fold in the walnuts.

5 Pour the batter into the baking pan and bake for 30 minutes, or until the top is golden and a toothpick inserted in the center comes out clean.

6 Meanwhile, prepare the syrup. Into a medium saucepan, place the water, sugar, cinnamon stick, lemon rind, and cloves. Bring to a boil, stirring to dissolve the sugar. Reduce the heat, cover, and simmer for 10 minutes. Strain the syrup to remove the cinnamon stick, lemon rind, and cloves.

7 Remove the cake from the oven and let it stand for 5 minutes. Poke about a dozen holes in the top with a toothpick and slow-

ly pour the warm syrup evenly over the cake. Let cool before cutting and serving.

Health Benefits

It's all about the walnuts. There is very strong evidence that walnuts can lower cholesterol levels and help reduce the risk of heart disease and diabetes. They may also boost your immune system, lower your blood pressure as well as your risk of stroke, improve your memory, and strengthen your urinary tract. Walnuts might have anti-inflammatory properties as well, making them good for arthritis, and some reports suggest they provide protection from macular degeneration and cancer.

Start-to-Finish
50 minutes

Do I Have What It Takes?
You'll need a 9-inch square baking pan and a box grater or lemon zester.

Shopping List
flour ▪ baking powder ▪ baking soda ▪ cinnamon ▪ canola oil ▪ sugar ▪ eggs ▪ orange ▪ milk ▪ walnuts ▪ cinnamon stick ▪ lemon ▪ whole cloves

This is one of my favorite pictures, maybe because mauve is my favorite color.

I bought the dishes at T.J. Maxx, and the white plate is actually a saucer. The

shine on top of the cake was hard to capture but I finally got it . . . after about

four hours.

Pink Grapefruit Cake

Pink grapefruit is the sweetest of them all and is also the highest in antioxidants. It's fun to make this cake and have people guess what's in it. The flavor is subtle but delicious, and they'll be asking for seconds. Be sure to scrub the fruit well before grating the zest, which you can do with a box grater, Microplane zester, or a hand-held lemon zester. Always grate the zest before juicing and be sure to save a little extra juice for the frosting. Once the frosting is done, you can drink any leftover juice for a nice blast of antioxidants.

1 1/2 cups all-purpose flour

1/2 teaspoon baking powder

1/2 teaspoon baking soda

1/8 teaspoon salt

1/4 cup low-fat buttermilk

1/4 cup fresh grapefruit juice

2 tablespoons unsalted butter, softened

2 tablespoons canola oil

3/4 cup sugar

2 large eggs

3/4 of the zest of 2 large pink grapefruits

GRAPEFRUIT CREAM CHEESE FROSTING

1 ounce regular cream cheese

1/2 tablespoon unsalted butter, softened

1 cup confectioners' sugar

1/4 of the grapefruit zest (leftover from the cake)

1/4 teaspoon vanilla extract

1 to 2 tablespoons grapefruit juice, to soften

1. Preheat the oven to 350°F. Lightly grease an 8-inch round cake pan with butter.

2. Into a bowl or onto waxed paper, sift together the flour, baking powder, baking soda, and salt.

3. In a small bowl or measuring cup, combine the buttermilk and grapefruit juice.

4. In a mixing bowl using an electric mixer on medium speed, beat the butter and oil. Slowly add the sugar and then the eggs, 1 at a time. Continue beating for 5 minutes, scraping down the sides of the bowl once. Stir in 3/4 of the zest, saving 1/4 of it for the frosting. With the mixer on the lowest speed, alternate adding the flour mixture and the buttermilk mixture, starting and ending with the flour mixture. This should take about a minute.

5. Pour the batter into the cake pan. Bake for 25 to 30 minutes, or until a toothpick inserted in the middle comes out dry. Cool in the pan.

6. Meanwhile, prepare the frosting. In a small bowl using an electric hand mixer, beat the cream cheese and butter. Mix in the confectioners' sugar, remaining grapefruit zest, and vanil-

la. Add enough juice to make a spreadable consistency. Cover the top of the cooled cake with the frosting.

Health Benefits

Besides this cake being low in fat, especially saturated fat, the anti-aging zest of grapefruit helps detoxify the body and can protect against cancer. The juice that's in the cake as well as the leftover juice you will probably drink can also protect against prostate cancer and macular degeneration, and boost your immune system.

Start-to-Finish
45 minutes plus cooling and frosting time

Do I Have What It Takes?
You'll need an 8-inch round cake pan and a box grater, Microplane, or hand-held lemon zester.

Shopping List
flour ▪ baking powder ▪ baking soda ▪ buttermilk ▪ pink grapefruits ▪ unsalted butter ▪ canola oil ▪ sugar ▪ eggs ▪ cream cheese ▪ confectioners' sugar ▪ vanilla extract

What a beautiful plate this is. I found it at a store that specialized in vintage china and managed to show off the ripples by reflecting light on it from behind. That also gave me a beautiful shine on top of the cake. The frosting was just starting to melt from the hot lights.

Parsnip Spice Cake

Parsnips don't get much respect, but they're even sweeter than carrots. Think of this as a spice cake with a streusel topping. Grating vegetables by hand is no fun, but here's a hint: The outer part of the parsnip is softer and much easier to grate, so buy a big one and save the inner core for my Chicken Soup (see page 68). For the best texture, use a box-style grater and do it in shifts, before your shoulder starts cramping.

1 1/2 cups all-purpose flour

1 teaspoon baking powder

1/2 teaspoon baking soda

1/2 teaspoon cinnamon

1/4 teaspoon mace
  (or nutmeg)

1/8 teaspoon ground ginger

1/8 teaspoon ground cloves

1/8 teaspoon salt

1/3 cup low-fat buttermilk

3/4 teaspoon vanilla extract

1/3 cup canola oil

2/3 cup sugar

2 large eggs

3/4 cup lightly packed grated
  parsnip (1 large or 2 small
  parsnips)

1/2 cup finely chopped pecans

TOPPING

1/3 cup finely chopped pecans

2 tablespoons lightly packed
  light brown sugar

1 tablespoon unsalted butter,
  softened

1 tablespoon sweetened
  flaked coconut

1 Preheat the oven to 350°F. Lightly grease an 8-inch round baking pan with butter.

2 Into a bowl or onto waxed paper, sift together the flour, baking powder, baking soda, cinnamon, mace, ginger, cloves, and salt.

3 In a small bowl or a measuring cup, combine the buttermilk and vanilla.

4 In a large mixing bowl using an electric mixer on medium speed, beat the oil while slowly adding sugar, then add the eggs, 1 at a time. Continue beating for 3 minutes, scraping down the sides of the bowl once. With the mixer on the lowest speed, alternate adding the flour mixture and buttermilk, then stir in the grated parsnip and pecans.

5 Pour the batter into the baking pan and bake for about 35 minutes, or until a toothpick inserted in the center comes out clean. Cool in the pan 5 minutes. Raise the oven rack and set the oven to broil.

6 In a small bowl, mix together the topping ingredients with a fork. Spread the topping on the cake and broil for 1 to 2 minutes, watching carefully not to burn. It browns quickly so don't take any phone calls!

Health Benefits

Research indicates that both parsnips and pecans may strengthen your immune system and protect against high cholesterol, heart disease, diabetes, and cancer. Pecans may also improve your skin and protect against macular degeneration and memory loss.

Kitchen Tip

Store Flour and Nuts in Your Freezer

Whole-grain flours and nuts can spoil quickly, especially during the summer. Store them in airtight containers in the freezer.

Start-to-Finish
1 hour

Do I Have What It Takes?
You'll need an 8-inch round baking pan and a box grater.

Shopping List
flour ▪ baking powder ▪ baking soda ▪ cinnamon ▪ mace (or nutmeg) ▪ ginger ▪ cloves ▪ buttermilk ▪ vanilla extract ▪ canola oil ▪ sugar ▪ eggs ▪ parsnip ▪ pecans ▪ brown sugar ▪ unsalted butter ▪ sweetened flaked coconut

I was feeling artistic with this photo. Can you tell that none of the plates match exactly? I scoured the house for all the different colors I could find. Some had rims and some not, but at least they were all the same size . . . almost.

Pumpkin Snacking Cake

Believe it or not, canned pumpkin has even more beta-carotene than fresh, which is good news because preparing fresh pumpkin is no easy task. This cake makes a good snack since it's not too sweet but it's still sweet enough for dessert. I just love the combination of pumpkin and walnuts so I hope you're not allergic to nuts. In case you are, you could make it plain or substitute some mini chocolate chips, but you never heard that from me.

$1^1/_2$ cups all-purpose flour

2 teaspoons baking powder

1 teaspoon baking soda

$^3/_4$ teaspoon cinnamon

$^1/_2$ teaspoon nutmeg

$^1/_8$ teaspoon ground cloves

$^1/_4$ teaspoon salt

$^3/_4$ cup canned pumpkin

$^1/_3$ cup 1% low-fat milk

$^1/_4$ cup canola oil

$^3/_4$ cup sugar

2 large eggs

$^1/_2$ cup finely chopped walnuts

Powdered sugar (optional), for dusting

Start-to-Finish
1 hour

Do I Have What It Takes?
You'll need a 9-inch round baking pan.

1 Preheat the oven to 350°F. Lightly grease a 9-inch round baking pan with butter.

2 Into a bowl or onto waxed paper, sift together the flour, baking powder, baking soda, cinnamon, nutmeg, cloves, and salt.

3 In a small bowl, whisk together the pumpkin and milk.

4 In a large mixing bowl using an electric mixer on medium speed, beat the oil while slowly adding the sugar. Add the eggs, 1 at a time, and continue beating until nice and thick, 5 minutes. With the mixer on the lowest speed, alternate adding the flour mixture and pumpkin mixture, beginning and ending with the flour mixture. When they are almost combined, fold in the walnuts.

5 Pour the batter into the baking pan and spread it evenly. Bake for 40 minutes, or until the top is a rich golden brown. Let it cool completely in the pan. You can dust it with powdered sugar or serve it plain.

Health Benefits

Walnuts are believed to lower the risk of heart disease and diabetes. They may also lower your blood pressure and triglycerides, improve your memory, strengthen your urinary tract, and help control your weight. Both walnuts and pumpkin may strengthen your immune system and protect you from macular degeneration and cancer. Pumpkin is also believed to support lung health.

Shopping List
flour ▪ baking powder ▪ baking soda ▪ cinnamon ▪ nutmeg ▪ cloves ▪ canned pumpkin ▪ milk ▪ canola oil ▪ sugar ▪ eggs ▪ walnuts ▪ powdered sugar (optional)

The cake stand was half-price at a store going out of business. I loved that. And that white plate with the crumbs was not in the plan but I happened to set it down after my necessary "testing" of the cake and decided to leave it there.

Desserts You Can Live With

Mixed Berry Cobbler MAKES 6 TO 8 SERVINGS

This is one of the best things to do with fresh summer berries. That's when berries are the sweetest and they won't come with a loan application. Examine all the berries well and toss out any that are moldy or just goopy. Wash and spread them on paper towels to dry. I used a mixture of blueberries, strawberries, blackberries, and raspberries but peaches can be substituted for one of the berries when they're in season. Leave all berries whole, even strawberries except for large ones, which should be quartered. Combining the fruit mixture just before baking helps keep it from creating too much juice.

TOPPING

1 cup all-purpose flour

$1/4$ cup sugar, plus extra for sprinkling

1 teaspoon baking powder

$1/2$ teaspoon baking soda

$1/8$ teaspoon salt

2 tablespoons cold unsalted butter

$2/3$ cup low-fat buttermilk

1 large egg

$1/2$ teaspoon vanilla extract

FRUIT MIXTURE

5 cups mixed berries

$1/3$ cup sugar

3 tablespoons cornstarch

1 Preheat the oven to 375°F.

2 To make the topping, in a medium bowl, sift together the flour, sugar, baking powder, baking soda, and salt. Cut the butter in with a pastry cutter or by using 2 knives until the mixture resembles coarse crumbs.

3 In a small bowl or measuring cup, combine the buttermilk, egg, and vanilla.

4 To make the fruit mixture, place the berries in a large bowl. In a small bowl, combine the sugar and cornstarch and add to the berries, stirring gently to combine.

5 Transfer the berry mixture into a 9-inch round baking pan. Pour the buttermilk mixture into the flour mixture and stir gently with a spoon until just combined. Spoon the topping onto the fruit in dollops. You do not need to cover all the fruit. Sprinkle the top with 1 to 2 teaspoons sugar.

6 Bake for 35 minutes, or until top is golden. Let cool slightly and serve warm, maybe with a little low-fat frozen vanilla yogurt.

Health Benefits

Nutritionally, a combination of mixed berries will give you the widest array of antiaging and health benefits. They may protect you against cardiovascular disease and cancer, as well as macular degeneration and cataracts. Their soluble fiber is recommended for diabetics, and they may also help prevent birth defects, Alzheimer's, and osteoporosis. Berries are also reported to strengthen the urinary tract, support the immune system, and preserve your memory. Maybe that's why they are often called "brain food."

Start-to-Finish
1 hour

Do I Have What It Takes?
You'll need a 9-inch round baking pan and a pastry cutter is helpful but not necessary.

Shopping List
flour ▪ sugar ▪ baking powder ▪ baking soda ▪ unsalted butter ▪ buttermilk ▪ egg ▪ vanilla extract ▪ fresh mixed berries ▪ cornstarch

For this picture I purchased a vintage linen tablecloth, plate, and cream & sugar set because it really suited an old-fashioned dessert like cobbler. I

wanted to put a little scoop of vanilla frozen yogurt next to the cobbler but it would

have melted too quickly.

Raspberry Tapioca

MAKES 4 SERVINGS

Tapioca pudding is one of the great old-fashioned desserts that you don't often see any more. In fact I usually have to search to find a box of tapioca in the grocery store. Be sure to shake the box before measuring and don't panic if the pudding seems too watery when it's done. It will solidify nicely when refrigerated. For company you can decorate this light-as-a-feather pudding with a bit of shaved chocolate on top.

2 cups 1% low-fat milk

$1/4$ cup quick-cooking tapioca

$1/3$ cup sugar

1 large egg

1 cup fresh raspberries

1 teaspoon vanilla extract

Start-to-Finish
10 minutes, plus 1 hour of refrigeration for chilling

Do I Have What It Takes?
No special equipment is needed.

Shopping List
milk ▪ quick-cooking tapioca ▪ sugar ▪ egg ▪ fresh raspberries ▪ vanilla extract

1   In a medium saucepan, whisk together the milk, tapioca, sugar, and egg. Let stand for 5 minutes. Bring to a boil over medium heat and cook, stirring, for 1 minute.

2   Remove from the heat and stir in the raspberries and vanilla. Pour into serving dishes and refrigerate for at least an hour before serving.

Health Benefits

Milk provides calcium for strong bones and teeth, and can help with hypertension. Raspberries may provide protection against heart disease, cancer, and memory loss as well as support for the immune system and urinary tract.

The dessert cup is from Anthropologie at the Grove in L.A., the spoon is from an antique shop in Studio City, California, and the background fabric is one of my sheer summer blouses. The result is a dreamy look for a dreamy dessert.

Orgasmic Rice Pudding

MAKES 2 SERVINGS . . . OKAY, SOMETIMES 1

Better than sex? Try this luscious pudding and see if you don't feel a little something. It's so rich tasting but is actually low in fat and super easy to make. Arborio rice makes the best pudding. For the lemon peel, just slice off a thin piece with a sharp knife. The only tricky thing is that this dish can easily spill over on the stove so keep an eye on the temperature. The burner should be just high enough to bubble. This pudding will thicken as it cools but it's good served either warm or cold. With or without the blueberries, mine never makes it to the fridge.

2 1/2 cups 1% low-fat milk

1/2 cup Arborio rice

1/4 cup sugar

1 cinnamon stick

1-inch piece of lemon peel

1/2 teaspoon vanilla extract

1/2 cup fresh blueberries
   (or 1/4 cup dried)

Start-to-Finish
35 minutes

Do I Have What It Takes?
No special equipment is needed.

Shopping List
milk ▪ Arborio rice ▪ sugar ▪ cinnamon stick ▪ lemon ▪ vanilla extract ▪ blueberries

1   In a medium saucepan, add the milk, rice, sugar, cinnamon stick, and lemon peel. Bring to a boil, stirring, until the sugar dissolves. Reduce the heat and cook, uncovered, at a gentle boil, stirring occasionally, until the rice is thick and creamy, about 25 minutes.

2   Remove the cinnamon stick and lemon peel. Stir in the vanilla and blueberries. Serve warm or refrigerate.

Health Benefits

With blueberries you may be getting protection for your heart with lowered cholesterol. Blueberries are also believed to support eye health and prevent birth defects, osteoporosis, senility, and cancer. Blueberries' other antiaging benefits may include a healthier urinary tract and brain as well as a stronger immune system and improved skin.

This vintage dessert cup was a great find and worthy of my Orgasmic Rice Pudding.

The cup went well with the striped plate that came from a "going out of business"

sale in Studio City, and the green background is one of my Gap T-shirts taped to

the back of a chair.

Tangerine Pudding Cake

MAKES 9 TO 12 SERVINGS

Can you tell I like comfort foods? If you can find tangerines in season with a nice thick and moist skin, you'll get a wonderful flavor with this pudding cake. If they are very small, you may need 2 tangerines. You'll also need a box grater or a Microplane zester, either of which creates a nice fine zest. If you use a little hand zester that produces long curly strips, they should be chopped into smaller bits. Remember to remove the zest from the tangerine and lemon before juicing them. You'll understand why if you ever forget. You'll need 2 baking pans, one that fits inside the other, because this cake needs a "water bath." This is truly a sort of pudding-cake combo that's fluffy-light and oh, so good.

$1/4$ cup all-purpose flour

$2/3$ cup plus 2 tablespoons sugar

$1/8$ teaspoon salt

1 cup low-fat buttermilk

Grated zest of $1/2$ lemon

Grated zest of 1 large tangerine

1 tablespoon fresh lemon juice

$1/4$ cup fresh tangerine juice

3 large eggs, separated

Start-to-Finish
1 hour

Do I Have What It Takes?
You'll need an 8-inch square baking pan and a larger baking pan to hold it, as well as a lemon zester, Microplane zester, or box grater. A whisk is helpful but not necessary.

1   Preheat the oven to 350°F. Lightly grease an 8-inch square baking pan with butter and place it inside a larger baking pan.

2   Into a large bowl, sift together the flour, $2/3$ cup sugar, and salt.

3   In another bowl, whisk together the buttermilk, lemon zest, tangerine zest, lemon juice, tangerine juice, and egg yolks. Add to the flour mixture, stirring with a whisk until smooth.

4   Put a quart of water on to boil.

5   In a medium bowl using an electric mixer on medium-high speed, beat the egg whites until foamy. Slowly add the remaining 2 tablespoons of sugar, beating until very stiff and glossy, about 5 minutes.

6   Using a spatula or "spoonula," gently stir $1/4$ of the egg whites into the cake batter. Gently fold in the remaining egg white mixture. Some small lumps of white are fine, and the batter will be thin.

7 Pour the batter into the baking pan and pour the hot water into the larger pan to a depth of about 1 inch. Bake for 30 to 35 minutes or until the cake springs back when touched lightly in the center. Serve warm or cooled.

Shopping List
flour ▪ sugar ▪ buttermilk ▪ lemon ▪ tangerine ▪ eggs

Health Benefits

Citrus fruits, especially the zest, are reported to have strong anti-aging properties. They may protect against cancer, heart disease, stroke, and macular degeneration. They may also support the lungs, urinary tract, and immune system and are good detoxifiers.

This beautiful antique plate was in my dining room hutch. Under it I put down a pink summer T-shirt from my closet and topped it with some sheer iridescent fabric. The lace-trimmed napkin is from my "company" linens that have never been used because people keep coming over with lipstick on.

Pomegranate Jelly

MAKES 4 SERVINGS

Boy, was I glad to hear that my favorite fruit is an antioxidant powerhouse. When pomegranates are not in season, I drink the juice, usually as a pomegranate spritzer, or I turn it into a fun dessert like this. You can also use some of the new combo juices like pomegranate-blueberry or pomegranate-mango. The best pomegranate juices are the ones sold at the health food store because they're low in sugar and are not filtered.

1 tablespoon unflavored gelatin (1 envelope)

2 cups cold pomegranate juice

Start-to-Finish
15 minutes, plus 3 hours of chilling time

Do I Have What It Takes?
No special equipment is needed.

Shopping List
unflavored gelatin ▪ pomegranate juice

1 In a medium bowl, sprinkle the gelatin over $^1/_2$ cup of the cold pomegranate juice and let stand for 5 minutes.

2 Heat the remaining $1^1/_2$ cups of juice until it's just below the boiling point. Add the juice to the bowl, stirring until the gelatin is dissolved. Pour into dessert glasses and chill for 3 hours before serving.

Health Benefits

In case you haven't heard, pomegranate juice has three times more polyphenols than red wine or green tea. It has anti-inflammatory properties and may be beneficial to asthmatics. It may also protect the arteries, immune system, and urinary tract, lower cholesterol, and help safeguard against memory loss and cancer.

For this vibrant dessert I looked for a matching background to bring out the beautiful

garnet color of the jelly. The rose fabric I chose was actually a cocktail dress that I made

to wear to a television syndication convention in New Orleans. I shot this picture outside,

and when the sun caught the jelly in the spoon, it seemed to change color, but I really

did scoop it out of the goblet.

Mango Mousse MAKES 4 SERVINGS

Here is an elegant dessert that looks great, tastes great, and does not feel heavy after a meal. Look for a ripe mango that gives when you lightly squeeze it. To get the most flesh from a mango, I remove the skin with a vegetable peeler and then slice away the fruit from every angle down to the stone, and I do it on a dinner plate to save all the juices. And as I say whenever there is lemon in a recipe, don't even think about using bottled lemon juice!

1 tablespoon plain gelatin (1 envelope)

$^1/_4$ cup cold water

1 large ripe mango, peeled and pit removed

$^1/_3$ cup sugar

8 ounces plain fat-free yogurt

1 teaspoon fresh lemon juice

$^1/_2$ teaspoon vanilla extract

$^1/_4$ cup heavy whipping cream

Start-to-Finish
40 minutes, plus 3 hours of chilling time

Do I Have What It Takes?
You'll need a food processor.

1 In a small saucepan, sprinkle the gelatin over the water and let stand for 5 minutes until dissolved.

2 Meanwhile, in a food processor fitted with a metal blade, puree the mango until smooth. Leave the pureed mango in the food processor bowl.

3 Place the saucepan containing the gelatin over medium heat and add the sugar and $^1/_4$ of the mango puree. Heat and stir until smooth, about 3 minutes. Set aside to cool (it will cool faster if transferred to a bowl).

4 In the food processor, combine the pureed mango with the cooled gelatin/mango mixture, yogurt, lemon juice, and vanilla, pulsing until just combined. Transfer to a bowl.

5 In a very small bowl with an electric hand mixer on medium speed, beat the whipping cream until you have firm peaks. Using a spatula, gently fold the whipped cream into the mango puree.

6 Transfer to dessert dishes and chill for at least 3 hours before serving.

Kitchen Tip

Whipping Cream in a Flash

Chill the bowl and beaters from your mixer beforehand and the cream will whip in less than a minute.

Health Benefits

The beta-carotene in mango could provide protection against cancer, particularly lung cancer, as well as heart disease, cataracts, and macular degeneration. Another of its antiaging benefits may be a stronger immune system.

Shopping List
plain gelatin ▪ mango ▪ sugar ▪ plain fat-free yogurt ▪ lemon ▪ vanilla extract ▪ heavy whipping cream

It took forever to get the reflections just right on this vintage plate, which I paired

with a Pyrex custard cup. The background is some leftover sewing fabric. I spent

more than three hours to get this picture and I love how it turned out.

Fruit Fantasy MAKES 8 TO 10 SERVINGS

Everyone will rave when you present this stunning and dramatic dessert. It's basically a giant cookie spread lightly with cream cheese and fruit, then glazed. It's best when assembled just before serving, but you can, and should, make the cookie ahead of time, and have your spread ready as well as your glaze. It's best to avoid hard fruits like apples or very soft ones like melon. Almost any jam or jelly you have on hand can be your glaze. Jelly should be heated slightly and jams mixed with a bit of water and strained if necessary. I like to use marmalade or apricot preserves. The first time I made this, I did not have a basting brush so I used the corner of a paper towel, dipping it in my glaze and then dabbing the fruit. We learn to make do.

COOKIE

2 cups all-purpose flour

1 teaspoon baking powder

$1/4$ teaspoon salt

$1/3$ cup unsalted butter, softened

$1/3$ cup canola oil

$1/2$ cup sugar

1 large egg

1 tablespoon milk

$3/4$ teaspoon vanilla extract

SPREAD

8 ounces reduced-fat cream cheese

2 tablespoons sugar

$1/4$ teaspoon vanilla extract

FRUIT

Try to use different colors like red berries, green grapes, kiwi, and papaya. For my photo I used 2 bananas,

1 Preheat the oven to 375°F. Lightly grease a flat 14-inch round baking sheet with butter.

2 To make the cookie, into a bowl or onto waxed paper, sift together the flour, baking powder, and salt. Set aside.

3 In a mixing bowl with an electric mixer on medium speed, cream the butter and oil for about a minute. Slowly add the sugar, then the egg, milk, and vanilla, beating until well blended, 2 to 3 minutes.

4 With the mixer on the lowest speed, add the flour mixture, mixing just until combined.

5 Pat the mixture $1/4$ inch thick onto the baking sheet. Prick all over with a fork. Bake for about 12 minutes until the edges are lightly browned. Cool completely.

6 To make the spread, in a small bowl using an electric hand held mixer on medium speed, beat the cream cheese, sugar, and vanilla until well combined.

7 Spread the cream cheese mixture on the cooled cookie. Decorate with fresh fruit and brush all over with the glaze. Serve within 1 to 2 hours, otherwise refrigerate.

Health Benefits

By using several different colors of fruit you could get a variety of health benefits. As pictured, you might get protection against heart disease, cancer, and osteoporosis. You could also benefit with a stronger immune system, stronger teeth and eyes, plus a better memory.

2 kiwis, 1 papaya, 1 box each of raspberries and blueberries, and a handful of grapes. Sliced bananas should be coated with lemon juice to keep from turning brown while you assemble.

GLAZE

$^1/_4$ cup marmalade diluted with 1 to 2 teaspoons of water, or any jelly heated a bit to soften

Start-to-Finish
25 minutes to make the cookie, 1 hour for it to cool (unless baked in advance), 30 minutes to assemble: total 2 hours

Do I Have What It Takes?
You'll need a flat 14-inch round baking sheet and a soft basting brush.

Shopping List
flour ▪ baking powder ▪ unsalted butter ▪ canola oil ▪ sugar ▪ egg ▪ milk ▪ vanilla extract ▪ reduced-fat cream cheese ▪ fruits of your choice ▪ marmalade or jelly

It was a hot August day when this picture came together. How else would I find such beautiful raspberries? Fruit fantasy always looks best with a brightly colored border, like raspberries or halved cherries.

Index

Pomegranate
    health benefits of, 200
    Pomegranate Dressing, 84
    Pomegranate Jelly, 200-201
Popcorn
    health benefits of, 99
    Nutty Caramel Corn, 98-99
Potatoes
    Chicken-Vegetable Stew,
        124-125
    Fish and Chips, 128-129
    health benefits of, 129, 154
    Mashed Root Vegetables,
        154-155
    Roasted Vegetables, 156-157
    Scrambled Eggs that Rock,
        24-25
Poultry. *See* Chicken; Turkey
Prunes
    Cholesterol Buster Cookies,
        162-163
    health benefits of, 163
    stewed, 16
Pudding cake, Tangerine Pudding
    Cake, 198-199
Puddings
    Orgasmic Rice Pudding,
        196-197
    Raspberry Tapioca, 194-195
Pumpkin
    health benefits of, 4, 47, 189
    Pumpkin Chocolate Chip
        Muffins, 46-47
    Pumpkin Snacking Cake,
        188-189

Q
Quesadilla, Black Bean, 112-113
Quick Breads
    Apple Breakfast Bread,
        40-41
    Banana Walnut, 44-45
    Jalapeño Corn Bread, 48-49

R
Radishes, Splendiferous
    Cruciferous Salad, 74-75

Rainbow Fried Rice, 114-115
Rapini
    Broccoli Bean Pasta, 102-103
    health benefits of, 103
Raspberries
    health benefits of, 33, 37,
        194
    Mixed Berry Cobbler,
        192-193
    Raspberry Tapioca,
        194-195
    Sweet Raspberry-Corn
        Muffins, 36-37
    Whole-Grain Waffles with
        Berries, 26-27
Red kidney beans
    Bean Salad, 76-77
    Turkey Chili, 104-105
Rice
    Broccoli, 136-137
    Chicken and Peppers,
        106-107
    Greek, 140-141
    Orgasmic Rice Pudding,
        196-197
    Rainbow Fried Rice,
        114-115
    Stuffed Peppers, 122-123
Roasted peppers. *See* Peppers,
    roasted
Roasted Vegetables, 156-157
Romaine lettuce, Antioxidant
    Slaw, 72-73
Rutabaga
    Chicken-Vegetable Stew,
        124-125
    Mashed Root Vegetables,
        154-155

S
Salad dressings
    Balsamic, 82
    Honey Mustard, 83
    Italian, 83
    Pomegranate, 84
Salads
    Antioxidant Slaw, 72-73
    Bean, 76-77

Beet, 78-79
    Splendiferous Cruciferous,
        74-75
    Tomato and Onion, 80-81
Salmon
    health benefits of, 110
    Salmon Patties, 110-111
Salsa
    Mango Salsa, 94-95
    Tomato Salsa, 88-89
Scallions
    Greek Rice, 140-141
    Tabouli, 142-143
    Tomato and Onion Salad,
        80-81
Scrambled Eggs that Rock, 24-25
Seven-Minute Creamy Carrots,
    148-149
Snacks
    benefits of snacking, 10
    healthy substitutions, 11
    Nutty Caramel Corn, 98-99
    Parmesan Tortilla Crisps,
        96-97
    See also Dips
Soups
    Beans 'n' Greens, 58-59
    Beet and Cabbage Borscht,
        66-67
    Black Bean, 62-63
    Chicken, 68-69
    Corn Chowder, 60-61
    Cream of Broccoli, 64-65
    Roasted Tomato, 56-57
    Vegetable Micro-Miracle,
        54-55
Spaghetti with Greens, 132-133
Spinach
    Antioxidant Slaw, 72-73
    Greek Rice, 140-141
    health benefits of, 5, 31, 134,
        140, 150
    Spinach Pesto, 134-135
    Spinach with Sweet Walnuts,
        150-151
    Superfood Scramble, 30-31
Splendiferous Cruciferous Salad,
    74-75
Stewed Prunes, 16